# SCHOOLWORKS:

## Reinventing Public Schools To Create the Workforce of the Future

Innovations in Education and Job Training
*From Sweden, West Germany,*
*France, Great Britain. . .*
*And Philadelphia*

William E. Nothdurft

**A German Marshall Fund of the U.S. Book**

The Brookings Institution
Washington, D.C.

**SchoolWorks: Reinventing Public Schools to Create the
Workforce of the Future**
Copyright © 1989 by The German Marshall Fund
   of the United States

The sources of photographs in this book are gratefully acknowledged: Page $x$—German Information Center. 10—Swedish Information Service. 28—Herbert Seiler. 44—French Youth Training Delegation. 56—Herbert Seiler. 74—University of Pennsylvania Publications Office. 84—WEPIC.

Cover design by Susan Foster
Typesetting by Edington-Rand, Inc., Riverdale, Maryland

The paper used in this publication meets the minimum requirements
of the American National Standard for Information Sciences—Permanence of Paper for Printed Library Materials, ANSI Z39.48-1984.

**A German Marshall Fund of the U.S. Book**
*Published by*
THE BROOKINGS INSTITUTION
*1775 Massachusetts Avenue, N.W.*
*Washington, D.C. 20036*

# CONTENTS

# FOREWORD

*On April 30, 1988, a small group of public school teachers, principals, and administrators from an economically distressed neighborhood on the western edge of Philadelphia boarded a jumbo jet bound for Gothenburg, Sweden—the first of several stops on a tour of some of the best education and training programs in some of the most troubled neighborhoods in Europe. Six months later, prompted by the imaginative proposals these educators produced as a result of their trip, another Philadelphia group—this time leading state and local policymakers—made a similar journey.*

*The travelers were all, directly or indirectly, participants in the West Philadelphia Improvement Corps (WEPIC)—one of the nation's leading local education and training initiatives. WEPIC is a rapidly growing partnership of public schools, institutions of higher education, local and state government agencies, community groups, and private businesses dedicated to a single concept: that public elementary and secondary schools can be the catalysts of projects to revitalize disadvantaged communities— projects that engage young people in education as they never have been before, build their self-esteem, provide them with practical and marketable skills, and give them, their parents, and their neighbors a new sense of purpose, a renewed sense of hope. In short, WEPIC is committed to the notion that schools can play a major role in creating the workforce of the future, even in the most disadvantaged neighborhoods in America.*

*The two trips to Europe—specifically, to Sweden, France, West Germany and Great Britain—were sponsored by the German Marshall Fund of the United States, a private American foundation. The trips were arranged so that the travelers might learn from successful programs underway abroad and so that they might share their experiences with educators and policymakers grappling with the same stubborn social and economic problems in Europe.*

*This report describes what they found. It also presents guiding principles for strengthening workforce competence in*

*America, with particular emphasis on those Americans who will make up an increasingly significant portion of our future workforce—young minorities and blacks from our most disadvantaged neighborhoods.*

*Since the German Marshall Fund began in 1972, it has sought to address problems common to industrialized societies, especially those problems most troubling to the Atlantic community. This has meant keeping watch for innovative solutions being pursued on one side of the Atlantic that might be adapted for use on the other. Just such an instance is provided by the European programs in education and job training that the two WEPIC groups observed. Fund Program Officer Anne Heald determined that many other Americans working to smooth the school-to-work transition would also like to expand their vision of what can be done. She collaborated with the Fund's director of communications, Elizabeth McPherson, to develop this volume.*

*Bill Nothdurft, the author, is a nationally recognized authority on economic development policy and an advisor to state governments and national associations. He has produced a compelling set of profiles of programs that are making public education more relevant to the world of work. Our hope is that these "success stories" will encourage other broadly based efforts to revitalize communities and schools.*

Frank E. Loy
President
The German Marshall Fund of the United States

# CHAPTER 1

# WORKFORCE COMPETENCE:
## Where Education
## and Economy Intersect

*The year was 1851, and in the elegant boardrooms of some of England's major industrial companies an edgy note of concern had crept into the conversations of the nation's business leaders. The source of this concern was the industrial exhibition at London's Crystal Palace, where American products were stealing the show. Mass produced at high levels of quality with interchangeable parts and sold at competitive prices, the American products had shaken the British manufacturers' accustomed positions of economic dominance in the Empire. Hurriedly, they mounted a fact-finding tour. What they discovered only deepened their worry: the secret of American manufacturing excellence wasn't better machinery or process innovations, but the high education level of the American workforce. In New England, then the nation's industrial heartland, 95 percent of adults could read and write, compared to just two-thirds in Old England. In subsequent years, history would record that Britain failed to close this talent gap and never recovered its industrial lead.[1]*

## The Competence Crunch

*"Development, of itself, does not create opportunity. . .opportunity is for the skilled."*

—Ron Leighton, Member of Parliament
for Newham Borough, East London

Much more than in 1851, global economic competitiveness is built upon the foundation of an educated and skilled workforce. Today, however, only perhaps 80 percent of our workforce is functionally literate. Moreover, America's future workforce will be drawn increasingly from the ranks of our least educated citizens. As a result, like Britain in the mid-1800s, our economy is suffering.

The suffering is not immediately obvious. The United States economy is producing new jobs at a prodigious rate—19 million in the past six years alone. But increasingly these jobs are going begging. In booming New England and in fast-growing communities and regions throughout the nation, labor shortages have emerged, threatening future growth potential.

Despite these shortages, there are people out there who need jobs, and their numbers are growing. They are young people who have dropped out of school and cannot find work. They are experienced workers whose skills are no longer in demand. They are single mothers with young children and few resources to care for them. They are predominantly minorities. They are increasingly immigrants. And they share one characteristic in common: they are the people least qualified for the work that is available. Their inability to secure work has been, until recently, principally a social issue. But it is no longer. They are our future workforce; their future is our future.

Several converging demographic trends—most notably the end of the postwar baby boom and the peaking of the entry of women into the workforce—have already begun to slow the rate of growth of America's labor force. By the 1990s, it will grow only half as fast as it did in the 1970s. In 1985, America's workforce was dominated by U.S.-born white males and females. They comprised 47 percent and 36 percent, respectively, of the total labor force. U.S-born nonwhite men and women each comprised only 5 percent of the labor force. Immigrant men and women represented only 4 and 3 percent, respectively, of the total.

But the picture changes dramatically as we look ahead. Only 15 percent of the new entrants to the labor force between 1985 and 2000 will be U.S.-born white males. U.S.-born white women will comprise 42 percent of the new entrants, U.S.-born nonwhite men and women 7 and 13 percent, respectively, and immigrant men and women 13 and 10 percent.[2]

This emerging workforce approaches the world of work with significant handicaps. A disproportionate number of the young people that are, or will soon be, entering the workforce come from families that are poor or headed by single parents who are themselves poorly educated and largely unskilled. These young people are three times more likely than others to drop out of school. Indeed, an estimated 700,000 young people—most of them minorities—drop out of school each year. In many American cities the dropout rate approaches 50 percent. Another approximately 700,000 young people complete high school but remain functionally illiterate. The working-age immigrants entering the country not only lack language skills but are generally poorly educated as well.[3]

At the same time, the skill requirements of the new jobs being created in our economy are increasing. Higher skill jobs are growing and low skill jobs are fast disappearing. Even the most basic service jobs have skill requirements higher than in the past—better verbal skills, different or more complex computational skills.

Caught in the middle of these two trends—decreasing skill levels and increasing skill requirements—is the American economy, and the strain is already showing. Employers are spending billions of dollars annually on remedial training just to make would-be employees work-ready. They complain not just that young people are poorly educated, but that they have little understanding of the world of work. For many young job applicants, this ignorance is understandable: they come from families where the experience of work is unusual rather than the norm, and they come from neighborhoods that most businesses abandoned long ago.

The growing mismatch between the quality of the workforce and the skill requirements of new jobs shows up in several ways. First, despite "Now Hiring" signs in virtually every shop window and thick "Help Wanted" sections in major newspapers, a significant portion of the working-age population—perhaps as many as 20 million people—remains out of the labor force.[4] They face many barriers, but perhaps the most daunting is that they lack the qualifications for even the most basic jobs.

Second, the economies of booming regions are bumping up against real labor shortages across a wide spectrum of job categories. The New England states, with some of the lowest unemployment rates and the most competitive industries in the nation, have begun to post below-average employment growth figures—a sure sign of labor shortages. Without trained workers, the region, and others like it around the country, will find it difficult to maintain economic momentum. In short, people have become the biggest constraint to future economic growth.

Third, despite the nation's spectacular job-creation rate, poverty levels persist at levels largely unchanged in decades and the gap between rich and poor is widening. This latter trend is connected directly to the worker-skill mismatch: too few qualified workers chasing too many high-skill jobs raises the wage rate for the better jobs, while too many low-skilled workers chasing too few low-skill jobs depresses the wage rate for the rest.

## Old World Solutions
## To New World Problems

*"We must create not a 'high tech' but a 'high skill' economy, through competence-building at all levels of education and business."*

—Allan Larsson, Director General
Swedish National Labor Market Board

The issue of workforce competence is not unique to the United States. It gnaws at the heart of every advanced industrial nation. The more complex the economy, and the more heterogeneous the population, the greater the problem. It is a central factor determining the national standings of the global economic competition, and there is not a single industrial nation that is not dissatisfied with the quality of the products of its education and worker training systems.

We are accustomed to comparisons, invariably unfavorable, between the skill levels of American and Japanese workers. But much closer to home, at least culturally, the industrialized economies of Western Europe are struggling with precisely the same workforce competence issues. More to the point, there is evidence that several are succeeding: with economies growing as fast or faster than our own, poverty rates are generally lower, there are far fewer people left outside the labor force, and worker productivity is high.

The reason is basic: many of these nations, capitalist and socialist alike, have an historical commitment to human investment as a fundamental economic principle, and the commitment is shared by government, business, and labor alike.

Beyond this historical commitment, there are several recent reasons for Europe's attention to workforce competence issues. First, the issue of global competitiveness—and thus the issue of workforce education and skill levels—emerged sooner in many European nations than in the United States because of their longstanding interest in export markets. Because of their small domestic markets, these nations traditionally have depended upon exports for growth to a greater degree than the United States. A few European countries, particularly West Germany and Sweden, saw that the secret to securing larger export market share was product quality, and that the secret to product quality was workforce quality—specifically, workers with relevant skills. Consequently, integration of the world of school and the world of work, already advanced in these countries, has accelerated during the past decade.

Second, the upcoming integration of product and service markets throughout the 12-nation European Community at the end of 1992 has given the workforce-skill issue new urgency. With protective barriers down, businesses that can claim that they have the best products, the best services, and—most important—the best workmanship, will gain market share, and the less skilled will lose. Consequently, each member nation is developing formal programs for producing universally recognized worker skill credentials.

Third, two decades ago, rapid economic growth in several Western European nations created significant shortages in low-skill labor categories. Workers willing to take low-paying (by European standards), low-skill production jobs were imported from Eastern Europe, Turkey, and North Africa, among other places, to take jobs Europeans were unwilling to take. Today, with skill levels increasing for even the most basic jobs, and with simmering social problems associated with these poor and poorly integrated "guest workers," education and skill-upgrading has taken on important social, as well as economic, importance—a situation not unlike that faced by many American cities.

Fourth, in a few European countries, there exists a palpable and universal acknowledgment of the centrality of work to the well-being of both the individual and the society as a whole. Consequently, active labor market measures designed to provide people with work are pursued before passive measures designed only to assure people of income support are applied. Thus, particularly in Sweden and West Germany, there is somewhat greater analytic and policy attention given to solving the root causes of unemployment and poverty than there is to simply ameliorating their effects. The result of that attention has been a universal interest in increasing workforce skill levels in general and in investing in the work-readiness of young people in particular.

A focal point for European efforts to upgrade workforce quality has been the relationship between schools (principally, but not exclusively, secondary schools) and the world of work.

Several European nations have developed both strong universal systems for assuring that all young people obtain an education that includes specific preparation for work, and special programs for disadvantaged individuals and groups, and in some cases distressed communities, that have "fallen through the cracks" of those universal systems. Both the universal and the special programs are designed to present young people with clear paths from school to work and a wide range of choices among these paths. Although many of these programs have been in place for years, today they are all in the process of being adapted systematically to meet the demands both of new segments of the population and of an increasingly competitive global economy.

The United States, in contrast, tends to excel in the category of special programs and demonstration projects—indeed, one of the most outstanding examples is profiled in these pages. The relative abundance of imaginative local approaches to school improvement, workforce skill development, community rehabilitation, and related issues is a natural outcome of our pluralistic heritage. At the same time, however, nationwide consensus on these issues, while growing, has so far eluded us, and large numbers of people are falling through the cracks between local initiatives. Unlike European societies, we have yet to turn growing national concern about workforce competence into coherent, universally available action programs capable of ensuring that school graduates are ready, willing, and able to enter and succeed in the working world.

## *Workforce Competence and Schools: The Essential Policy Questions*

At least part of the reason for this lack of clarity is the sheer size and diversity of the workforce-related issues the United States confronts: a wide array of ethnic minorities and a rapidly growing immigrant population, deep-seated and stubborn urban poverty problems, the need for comprehensive school reform, and more. They dwarf the problems faced by our European competitors which, in comparison, often have more homogeneous populations, less severe poverty conditions affecting smaller populations, and relatively effective secondary education systems.

On the other hand, it may well be that it is precisely because their problems are less overwhelming that the Europeans have found it easier to grasp the relationship between national economic competitiveness and workforce skill development. And although there are historical and social differences that affect both the kinds of solutions they have developed and their ability to be applied in the United States, the truth is that we share with Europe many common cultural, economic, and political values.

In the pages that follow, we profile how imaginative programs in four European countries are addressing the challenge of producing skilled, work-ready young entrants to the workforce, and how one pioneering American city is combining lessons learned in Europe with its own initiatives to reinvigorate its public schools, remotivate and build the skills of its young students, and rehabilitate an entire community.

Each of these profiles addresses aspects of four fundamental policy questions:

1. *How should education and job training systems be changed to produce skilled new entrants to the workforce?*
   European primary, secondary, and higher education systems are older and—theoretically, at least—should be more resistant to change than our own relatively young system. Yet in several countries these systems have been highly successful in meeting the workforce skill demands of a changing economy. Schools and workplaces have been drawn together and programs have been crafted to guarantee that non-university bound young people possess the knowledge and skills they need to secure rewarding work in growing, internationally competitive companies. How have they done it? What have been the keys to their success? What, if any, are the limits of the lessons we can learn from them?

2. *What are the institutional and political characteristics of the approaches that have been most successful at meeting these objectives?*

Despite class distinctions that still divide their populations, and political party systems that are sometimes more fragmented and more starkly polarized than our own, many European nations have crafted education and training programs that enjoy support across a broad political spectrum. How has that been accomplished? Are there principles so basic to human investment and economic progress that they transcend political ideology? How are those principles translated into institutional changes that are embraced by the institutions themselves?

3. *Who are the key players in creating effective education and training programs and what are their roles?*

It is one thing to say that everyone has a stake in upgrading workforce skills and improving the work-readiness of young entrants to the labor market, and quite another to provide them a seat at the table when decisions are made to translate these objectives into actions. Who are the critical stakeholders in education reform and workforce skill development and how are their interests best represented in both the design and implementation of new policy? Perhaps just as important, who should pick up the tab for strengthening workforce skills?

4. *How can a nation's universal public education systems be modified to ensure that skill-development opportunities are provided for the most disadvantaged individuals and distressed communities?*

Like the United States, European countries face a sharp decline in the number of young people entering the workforce in the next decade. To a significant extent, this fact alone drives efforts to ensure that every young person attending compulsory school has the skills necessary to secure rewarding work: they can afford to let no one fall behind. But the coming worker shortage also underscores the importance of specialized programs for reaching many other individuals on the fringes of every society—resident ethnic minorities, new refugees and immigrants, displaced workers, and the chronically unemployed and underemployed. Efforts to reach these segments of the population in some European countries have brought about a radical rethinking of the role of schools in training all members of a community, not just its children, and in rehabilitating entire neighborhoods. Which of these attempts has been most effective, and what characteristics are common to the most effective programs?

As we turn to the profiles themselves, it is important to remember that none of these countries has the related challenges of education reform, youth employment, workforce skill development, and revitalizing disadvantaged communities firmly in hand. Each is struggling to succeed, working within slightly different cultural and political environments, borrowing freely from each other, grappling with budget limitations, and trying to inject flexibility and a spirit of experimentation into traditionally inflexible institutions. There are lessons to be learned from each, and broader lessons to be learned from them all.

And yet there is a remarkable commonality of vision, startling in its simplicity: it is that *no nation can grow, economically or socially, without significant and sustained investments in the knowledge and skills of its people. . .all of its people.*

## Notes

1. Adapted from "Wanted: Human Capital," *Business Week*, September 19, 1988, pp. 100–101.
2. Hudson Institute data, reported in *Business Week*, op. cit., pp. 102–103.
3. Arnold Packer, "Retooling the American Worker," *Washington Post*, July 10, 1988, p. C-3.
4. Louis Uchitelle, "America's Army of Non-Workers," *New York Times*, September 27, 1987, Sec. 3.

# CHAPTER 2

# SWEDEN:
# A Nation Guarantees Its Children Work

*Everything about Gothenburg, Sweden is busy, industrious. At 6:00 a.m., as the thin morning light begins to penetrate the dense fog along the waterfront, the main fish auction is already over. Yesterday's catch is already graded, boxed, iced, and tagged for delivery to shops and restaurants throughout Europe. As the last of the fishing boats disappears downriver into the retreating mist, forklifts scurry around the docks loading cases of cod, herring, shrimp and more exotic North Sea fish into a steady stream of arriving and departing refrigerated trucks.*

*By 7:00, the construction cranes are swinging above the city—half of Gothenburg seems to be under construction or renovation. By 9:00, as buses and streetcars deposit successive waves of office workers and shopkeepers in Kungsportsplatsen, the central plaza, the din of heavy equipment is everywhere.*

*But across the harbor, things are quieter. Huge cranes stand silent watch over empty shipbuilding yards, awaiting business that comes less frequently every year. The passenger and general cargo ships Sweden once built have been replaced by efficient container ships and other specially designed vessels, many made in Korea. The huge drydocks of Gothenburg must be content with the occasional repair job.*

*Gothenburg is changing. Increasingly, traditional industries tied to the sea or the surrounding forests are being displaced by new industries. Gothenburg is the international headquarters of Volvo, of the SKF worldwide ball-bearing empire, of Hasselblad cameras, and of scores of other, smaller technology-driven industries with far-flung global markets. On the outskirts of the city, in the direction of the new international airport, busy commercial and light industrial developments are encroaching on tranquil farms whose red barns, steeply roofed white farmhouses, and thin rocky soil would make any New Englander feel at home.*

*On Hisingen Island, across the harbor from the city center,*
*in a century-old brick school building wedged among factories,*
*apartment blocks, and the shipyards, Sweden's school system is*
*adapting to the changes underway in the Swedish economy—*
*adapting with a wide array of training and education services*
*aimed at young people at risk of being left behind.*

## Blurring the Line
## Between School and Work

By U.S. standards, Sweden's low school dropout and youth unemployment figures are remarkable: fewer than 10 percent of all the students who complete compulsory school at age 16 fail to go on to upper secondary school for further education and training. The unemployment rate for young people age 16 through 24 is only 5 percent. Drugs, dropouts, teen pregnancy, and illiteracy are all single-digit issues.

There are several reasons these figures are so low. First, Sweden has an aggressive, nationwide labor market policy that emphasizes training and work experience (sometimes publicly subsidized) and relegates income maintenance to a last, and temporary, resort—a policy applied to young people with as much force as to adults.

Second, it is well-understood that post-compulsory education is the "passport" required for virtually all jobs. Roughly a decade ago, a population bulge released a relatively large number of 16 year-old compulsory school graduates to the labor market in the middle of a recession. With few jobs available, and rapidly increasing skill requirements for the jobs that were being created, youth unemployment grew sharply. To encourage young people to stay in school longer, and to respond to higher skill requirements as the economy picked up steam again, the Swedish government overhauled the nation's upper secondary school system, creating a comprehensive, integrated basic and vocational education system for 16 to 18 year-olds. By the mid-1980s the glut of young people entering the labor market had melted away, but because of the growing skill requirements of new jobs, completion of upper secondary school has become the new placement standard. Today, more than 90 percent of all compulsory school graduates go on to upper secondary education.

Third, and unquestionably most important, there is a deeply ingrained national consensus on the inseparability of education, work, and the good society that is held with equal conviction by all political parties and all segments of the society. In any year, fully 50 percent of all Swedish workers are involved in some kind of further education. Work is seen as the central defining element of one's life, and education is the means by which fulfilling work is secured and retained.

Consequently, the relationship between education and "Arbetsliv"—the Worklife—is a dominant theme in Swedish education:

> *Orientation to working life is a matter of urgency*
> *to everyone in school. It must be incorporated, in*
> *various forms, in the activities of schools from the*
> *first to the final grade, and in the actual*
> *transition from school to working life.*

—National Board of Education, April 1988

Experience with "Arbetsliv" begins in the first grade, at age seven. From then on, students spend from a few to several weeks each school year in public, commercial, and manufacturing workplaces. But the focal point of the school-to-work transition is the upper secondary school system. Upon completion of compulsory school at age 16, students in Sweden choose one of 27 "lines" or courses of study within six educational/occupational divisions in the upper secondary school system: arts and social sciences (liberal arts, music, etc.); the care professions (nursing, social services, etc.); economics and commerce (economics, trade, accounting, etc.); technology and science (production engineering, natural sciences, technology); technology and industry (process engineering, manufacturing, telecommunications, etc.); and agriculture, horticulture and forestry. These upper secondary lines currently range from two to four years in length, though a recent reorganization will soon make virtually all programs three years long.

Throughout upper secondary school, the line between education and job training is intentionally blurred. In addition to a "core" of Swedish, English, and Math, and coursework in their chosen line of study, students have industry-specific "worklife" experiences directly incorporated into the curriculum. Most upper secondary school students who do not plan to go on to college or university (only about 25 percent pursue higher education) will spend 10 to 20 percent of their time in work settings during their first and second year, and as much as 60 percent by their third year. Worklife experience is organized by vocational counselors in each school who are, in turn, advised by local vocational committees. The school system recruits businesses and labor unions to provide space and programs for these students. In turn, industry and labor advise schools about the education and skill requirements of the labor market and often negotiate the content of curricula.

At the sprawling international headquarters of SKF Industries, the extent to which this cooperative relationship can be taken is illustrated by an extraordinary on-site "industrial high school" for Gothenburg students who wish to pursue an industrial engineering career. Students pursue a core educational curriculum (Swedish, English, Math, etc.) as well as both theoretical and practical engineering and automation coursework. Teaching is handled by a university-certified head teacher whose salary is paid by the Gothenburg Education Department, and by two instructors per class group, provided by SKF. The program has an annual budget of 7 million Swedish Krona, of which the state provides only 1.5 million. SKF covers the balance of the program cost, in large part because it is ultimately the principal beneficiary: some 96 percent of the students go to work for SKF when they complete the program.

During their first year, these students spend most of their time in the school rooms established within the SKF complex and in the equipment rooms set aside for their use. As elsewhere in the Swedish upper secondary system, they spend a significant portion of their second year actually working—in this case, in the SKF factory. By their third year, they spend virtually all their time on the factory floor. Students are paid salaries during their second and third years and by the end of their second year generally know what job they will be offered when they finish their third year.

SKF's experience with the in-plant school has been so positive that they have expanded it to serve not just young people entering the labor market but existing adult employees who need to strengthen or upgrade their basic education levels or their specific skills. The result is even closer linkages between the educational system and industry. Indeed, headmasters of other upper secondary schools in

Gothenburg have come to realize that their teachers and courses have value to companies throughout the city and they are beginning to market educational services accordingly. In addition, several companies in the Gothenburg area have banded together to form a foundation designed to anticipate emerging skill needs. The foundation, working with the city school system, sells training programs to participating companies.

While a close relationship between school and work is traditional in Sweden, there is another motivation behind the experimentation currently underway: the competitiveness challenge of "1992"—the year the Common Market countries (of which Sweden is not a member) propose to fully integrate their product and service markets. Sweden's well-educated workers are already among the most productive in Europe (with a GDP one and a half times the EEC average). But the importance of credentials—of universally recognizable worker qualifications—is crucial to Sweden's ability to compete in the new economic environment that 1992 represents. And it must compete successfully: roughly half of Sweden's production workforce produces for export, and many of the rest produce for domestic markets in which there are international competitors.

To ensure that the productivity and competitiveness of the workforce is maintained, the content of upper secondary school coursework is changing slightly. Though worklife connections continue to predominate, broader skills in reading and calculating are being emphasized in the second and third years to assure workers who are literate as well as skilled, and who are flexible enough to adapt to rapidly changing labor market requirements.

### Sweden's "Youth Guarantee"

Of course, not all graduates of Sweden's compulsory schools pursue further education through the upper secondary school system. The relatively regimented character of mainstream Swedish education creates pressures for conformity that some young people are unwilling to accept. Others, for any of a number of reasons, may be unable to go on to upper secondary. Still others begin upper secondary school, find it irrelevant or incompatible with their needs, and drop out. Whatever their reasons, these young people—between 5 and 10 percent of the nation's 16 year-olds—quickly discover that they are virtually unemployable.

They are unemployable for two reasons. The first is cultural: education is so ingrained as a prerequisite to good citizenship in Sweden that anyone who has not completed upper secondary school is seen as incomplete. The second reason is economic: there simply are not many jobs available in the Swedish economy for new entrants who lack basic educational credentials and work experience. Between 1980 and 1987, for example, the percentage of available jobs for which some higher education and/or work experience was required increased from 65 percent to 75 percent. Within manufacturing, the figure rose from 48 to 67 percent.

Consequently, to augment its highly successful universal education programs, Sweden has developed a number of innovative special programs. In 1980, the Swedish Parliament concluded that while education was the solution to the problem of increasing rates of youth unemployment and long-term welfare dependency, it was also, in effect, part of the problem. While the mainstream route from preschool through compulsory school and on to upper secondary school seemed to suit more than 90 percent of the nation's children, it was so inflexible that the 10 percent who failed to go on to upper secondary school, or who subsequently dropped out, essentially were left behind. Moreover, it appeared to serve inadequately a relatively small but growing population of immigrants and refugees clustered in a number of Swedish communities.

Accordingly, to assure that no individual would be left behind, Sweden's Parliament established a "Youth Guarantee," decreeing that municipalities—specifically, local school authorities—would henceforth be held legally responsible for keeping track of, and finding education and work opportunities for, every young person between the ages of 16 and 18 not in upper secondary school—some 15,000 young people nationwide.

While some Swedish municipalities elected to pursue this responsibility through the conventional upper secondary school system, many concluded that the solution required a different educational approach. Gothenburg has been a leader in this regard and has established a variety of educational alternatives designed to reach and help every young person in the city, no matter how disadvantaged or disaffected. The pages that follow explore several of these special programs.

## *"A Long Deep Breath"—The Youth Centre Program*

*Lill Backlund is on the phone, recruiting. Working from a list of names provided by the city school system, she checks in with Michael, who dropped out of upper secondary school in Gothenburg last term. In an easy, concerned voice she asks how he is doing, whether he's found work. He has not. For the second time in several months, she invites him to the Youth Centre in Hisingen, one of three serving the city. He says he doesn't know what he wants to do, but that he knows he doesn't want to go back to school. She says she understands. He dismisses her: "You don't know what it's like." She says calmly, but firmly, that she knows because she dropped out herself. And besides, the Youth Centre isn't like school. You set your own goals, try out some of the jobs you've wanted but couldn't get into, strengthen your basic skills—and you get paid for it. He hesitates, then relents. He'll come by in the morning, just to check it out. She hangs up, turns, and smiles: "Sometimes all they need is a long, deep breath."*

The premise behind the Youth Centre Program is simple and pragmatic: not all young people respond to standardized public education the same way. Young people choose not to go on to upper secondary school, or drop out, or do poorly often for perfectly rational reasons—not because they are either delinquent or deficient. They look at the world around them and see little connection between what teachers want from them and what they themselves imagine they will need in the future. They lack vision for themselves, confidence in themselves, or simply information on the possibilities available to them. Sometimes they are simply not ready.

The goal of Gothenburg's three Youth Centres is to strengthen the basic skills and self-esteem of the 1,400 young people they serve so they are motivated to complete formal education, or are able to find fulfilling work. The Youth Centres, which are staffed by teachers, career counselors, a social worker, and a nurse, serve both the disadvantaged (immigrants, refugees, children in difficult family situations) and the disaffected (dropouts, poor students). While the principal objective of the Youth Centre is to ensure that these young people have the opportunity to pursue either further education or work, they also serve as a single point of access to health care, welfare services, and other forms of public assistance.

Young people who come to the Centres, either because they were recruited under the nationally mandated follow-up program or through word-of-mouth, begin by meeting with a career counselor and drawing up their own plan, with staff help. They take a basic skills test in Swedish, English, and Math and are advised on areas where additional study may be important to the goals in their plan. (For immigrants and refugees, civics and other aspects of Swedish life are also provided.)

To a degree which may seem unusual in a country known for the homogeneity of its culture and its commitment to democratic socialism, Youth Centres are designed explicitly to recognize, deal positively with, and even encourage the differences among individuals. Young people who, for whatever reason, seem not to "fit" within the upper secondary school system may choose among a wide array of alternative Youth Centre-run programs:

- **On-the-Job Training**: They may try working briefly at several different kinds of jobs, to help them choose a direction for themselves. While they participate, they will normally attend academic classes one day a week at the Youth Centre and be paid the equivalent of $400 per month, less taxes and expenses, by the Youth Centre.

- **Vocational Courses**: They can pursue vocational training in such areas as the restaurant business, health care, and building and construction, among others, and continue to be paid by the Youth Centre.

- **Pursue Studies**: They may pursue academic studies more intensively than one day a week if they wish, generally in preparation for a return to upper secondary school.

- **Youth Training Scheme**: They can obtain a full-time position for six months as assistants to employees in participating companies—a kind of longer-term on-the-job training program. They are entitled to one day a week of academic study at the Youth Centre or at the adult education facility where they work (should one exist) and are paid by their employer.

- **Apprenticeship Training**: In fields where labor is tight or vocational courses do not exist (such as building and construction trades, office work, or craft trades), Youth Centre members may participate in formal, two-year apprenticeship training programs—the equivalent of upper secondary education completion, but conducted by an employer. Salaries are paid in accordance with the apprenticeship agreement.

- **Youth Craft Workshop**: For those interested in pursuing craft careers, the Youth Centre program runs a separately housed workshop where woodworking, metalworking, and textile skills can be developed. Young people who choose this option receive personal and career counseling and take academic courses much as they would in a Youth Centre, and are paid by a Youth Centre.

- **Youth Printshop**: In a similar manner, the Youth Centre program operates a professional printshop in which students can learn both the skills of printing and the requirements of business management. Assisted by instructors, young people produce brochures, catalogues, and advertising materials for nonprofit associations and local government offices, in the process learning layout, production, photography, customer development, and business accounting and billing. Once a week, the students pursue academic studies in Swedish and math.

The results of the Youth Centre Program are impressive. Roughly a third return to school, having received at the Youth Centre the equivalent of the first year of upper secondary education. Another third enter the labor market, pursuing careers they began at the Youth Centre. A further 10 percent register with the Employment Service in pursuit of work in their chosen careers. The remaining 20 percent include those students who have moved out of the city or have begun families, and a small percentage who have failed to be helped by the Youth Centre.

What seems to make the difference for Youth Centre participants is the personal attention they receive and the flexible, experimental nature of the program which, taken together, give these young people an opportunity to find a niche for themselves in Swedish adult society.

In the process of working with the young people for which the community and the school system are legally responsible, the Youth Centres find some who need more intensive attention than the Youth

Centres can offer. For these young people, the Youth Centres have developed three special programs, described below.

### "Humlan": Intensive Care
### For the Emotionally Disadvantaged

*"Humlan" is Swedish for "bumblebee"—an insect
so heavy, in relation to its gossamer wings, that
technically it should not be able to fly. . .but
somehow does.*

Occasionally, Youth Centre staff in Gothenburg come across a child whose inability to perform either in school or on the job stems principally from emotional trauma—abandonment, abuse, family alcoholism or drug abuse, and the like—trauma so profound that even the innovative programs available at Youth Centres cannot lift them from the despair and "learned helplessness" in which they are imprisoned.

The Humlan Centre was establish six years ago as a kind of "place of last resort" for these alienated, socially isolated young people, who range in age from 16 to 20. As with the Youth Centres, the approach is gentle, and participation is voluntary. The staff of Humlan—five social workers and two teachers to serve an average of 40 young people—will typically arrange two preliminary meetings with young people referred to them by the Youth Centres. The first is designed simply to explain to the student that there is a place for them where people will understand their special circumstances. The second meeting begins to explore their needs and interests, both in terms of education and work.

If they decide to participate, Humlan offers four kinds of services, with the precise level of emphasis tailored to individual cases: basic educational skill development (Humlan students typically have 5th or 6th grade reading levels on entry); work experience (helping them identify and try their "dream jobs," building confidence slowly through direct experience); therapy sessions (a minimum of one session per week, but often more frequently); and family counseling/social support (to help them cope with, or extract themselves from, the situations from which they came). At an annual cost of 500,000 Swedish Krona, the program is relatively costly and staff-intensive. But Gothenburg officials see the cost as a long-term investment designed to offset future social costs.

## *Grimas Farm:*
## *Intensive Care for the Most Disaffected*

*The experience of driving a tractor or handling a horse gives city dropouts a sense of knowing something their friends don't know—a sense of power. . .and the confidence to start over again.*

—Erik Ivarsson, teacher, Grimas Farm School

Several years ago, a Gothenburg school headmaster concluded that the city's upper secondary school dropouts were not so much academically incapable as they were educationally disaffected, and that the root cause of that disaffection was a kind of "learned helplessness"—a profound sense of failure and lack of self-esteem. He persuaded city officials to donate a farm on the outskirts of town to serve as a "learning-by-doing" alternative school.

Today the farm serves as a kind of "proving ground" for an average of 12 city teenagers between the ages of 16 and 18. Under the guidance of three teachers, the young people work 40 hours per week (commuting to the farm daily by bus) for a full year—through all four farm seasons—raising livestock (pigs, cows, and horses), growing both feed and greenhouse crops, and doing the full range of chores, from cleaning out the barns to repairing tractors and other farm machinery. Ten hours each week are spent on classroom studies (Swedish, math, science) and on special projects—most recently, a geological and political history of the valley in which the farm is situated. Should they require them, personal and family therapy sessions are arranged.

The farm-related work is designed to provide both immediate application of basic academic skills and multiple opportunities for the students to prove themselves, build confidence, and develop self-esteem. Few of the graduates of Grimas Farm choose agricultural careers. That isn't the point. The objective is to provide, through the daily responsibilities of running the farm, experiences that will help them believe in themselves and, as a result, give them the confidence to return to school.

## The Wendelsberg Folk High School Project: Alternative Education for "Square Pegs"

*Question: How do children who go into school with their eyes big with anticipation become, by age 16, tired and alienated? Answer: Because the schools show them over and over again what their weaknesses are, how they don't measure up. Soon they come to believe it.*

—Karle Hill, co-director, Folk High School Project, and 1987 Teacher of the Year

For a significant number of those who do not go on to upper secondary school, or who drop out from it, the problem is not lack of interest in learning, but frustration with the structure or the content of conventional schooling. They may be bright, even inquisitive, but their need for individualized ways of learning cannot be accommodated by standardized instruction. They are "square pegs." For them, school provides daily reinforcement of not fitting, not measuring up.

Two years ago, as a spinoff of the Youth Centre Program, Gothenburg provided yet another alternative education program for its dropouts—a program for young people age 18 to 25 operated out of the Wendelsberg Folk High School, a residential adult education facility situated some 20 km outside of the city. Folk high schools, a 125 year-old tradition in Sweden, are independent alternative colleges where any Swedish adult can pursue further education. Roughly half are run under the auspices of various popular movements (labor unions, churches, associations), the other half by municipalities and county councils. Their format and educational emphases vary, though all must provide a basic core curriculum in Swedish and English.

The experimental program at Wendelsberg gives Gothenburg's "square pegs"—including young people who may have gone through the farm program or Humlan—the opportunity to craft their own syllabus and pursue it at their own pace, with the guidance of an advisor. On the first day of the term, students decide on the subjects they want to pursue (beyond the core curriculum) and display their proposed syllabus along with those of other participating students, so that others may sign up as well. They may pursue their studies independently or in small classes guided by an advisor, but in all cases they must "bring it back to the group"—present the results of their studies to other students in the project.

The new course is the equivalent of the first year general course at the Folk School. Students who complete the program satisfactorily may then join the Folk School proper in the second year, obtaining high school certificates in the course they have taken. As with other Youth Centre-related programs, students participating in this experimental program are paid approximately $400 per month (less taxes and expenses) by the Youth Centre from which they were referred.

## The Swedish Context:
## An Active Labor Market Policy

Sweden's success at smoothing the transition from school to work, even for disadvantaged or disaffected young people, is due in large measure to the pervasive influence of the fundamental cornerstone of Swedish economic and political life: its active labor market policy. Stated in starkest terms, the guiding principle is this:

*Don't guarantee people income;*
*guarantee them a job.*

Sweden is dedicated to achieving full employment with low inflation. It accepts no percentage of unemployment as either inevitable or unavoidable. Given the centrality of work as the defining element of life in Swedish culture, working—whether in a private sector, public sector, or subsidized job—is always preferable to not working. Thus, as a matter of policy, "active" measures—retraining and job creation—will always be taken before such "passive" measures as income maintenance.

Sweden's "social partners"—government, business, and unions—have spent decades developing an economic system designed to achieve the dual goals of this labor market policy. The system rests on three policy assumptions. First, no matter how strong the economy, no matter how high the labor demand, there will always be some people the economy won't reach without active measures. Second, if company profits are allowed to rise to unreasonable heights, wage demands will rise as well, creating inflation. Third, there should be wage solidarity—equal pay for equal work. Companies unable to pay fair wages are, by definition, uncompetitive; they should make way for those who can.

The "work strategy" is the driving force in this system, and there are two components to the operational mechanism that makes it work: the Employment Service (operated by the National Labor Market Board) and the Training Service (operated by the National Employment Training Board). The Employment Service, a government agency, fills more than 75 percent of all public and private vacancies in the nation and, through a network of neighborhood and "storefront" job centers, meets the placement needs of 80 percent of the nation's unemployed. The Employment Service also manages a variety of "labor market demand measures"—publicly subsidized or created part-time jobs, temporary "youth team" jobs for young people 18 to 20 years old, "employability institutes" for people with special needs or handicaps, and enterprise start-up grant programs, among others. Cash unemployment grants are provided only as a last resort, and even then only temporarily.

The Training Service, a self-supporting government-owned corporation, packages and sells training services both to the Employment Service and to private employers. About 80,000 individuals receive training each year, delivered through a network of 100 training centers. Roughly 20 percent of the curriculum is basic remedial education; the balance includes hundreds of individual professions. Trainees receive government grants equal to 91 percent of their former wages while they are in training. The modular nature of the course components permits the Service to tailor training to each individual's competence and experience.

While the Employment Service/Training Service system principally serves adults, it has a direct relationship—both philosophically and operationally—with the upper secondary school system and such municipal follow-up programs as the Youth Centres. While 60 percent of the new labor force each year comes from the adult labor market training program, fully 40 percent comes from school graduates. In fact, education and job training are a continuum in Sweden. Graduates from upper secondary schools and Youth Centres pass out of the sphere of the education system and into the sphere of the labor market system relatively smoothly. Changes in the needs and expectations of employers mean that the educational system is in a constant state of fine-tuning. Indeed, the modular structure of the Training Service's courses is currently being introduced in the structure of upper secondary education to make the transition from school to work even smoother.

### Lessons from Sweden

Sweden's consistently innovative social policies are often discounted by other nations as being somehow peculiar to Sweden— not transferable outside the context of that nation's aggressively capitalistic brand of socialism. But while there are differences in both cultural history and political approach between Sweden and the United States, the underlying causes of illiteracy, youth unemployment, and school dropout problems are fundamentally the same. Imaginative, and often quite economically efficient, Sweden's education and youth employment initiatives present important lessons for other countries:

1. **The key to improving the school-to-work transition, decreasing the dropout rate, and producing a work-ready workforce, is creating an educational system with an explicit and gradually increasing work experience component.** In the absence of linkages to the working world, education becomes abstract and flirts with irrelevance. Unable to make the connection between what they are being taught and the world around them, many students tune out at an early age and drop out as soon as they have the opportunity. The more disadvantaged the student, the more this will seem a rational decision. The way to smooth the school-to-work transition is to make it as seamless as possible, by bringing the world of work into the classroom early in a student's school career.

2. **In both education and policymaking, patience is a virtue.** Sweden recognizes that even the strongest universal education

system will not reach everyone. Committed to the notion that every individual can and should contribute to the society, Sweden patiently seeks the right match between individual needs and public purposes. Thus, it crafts its alternative education and training programs so that they are varied and flexible, based on the belief that, in time, young people and good programs will find the right fit. Perhaps more important, Sweden is also patient in the development and implementation of national education and training policy—testing innovations, giving them time to work, evaluating and retesting, and eventually applying them nationwide. It prefers step-wise incremental adjustments to frequently shifting grand schemes.

3. **A "school" can be anything or anyplace you want it to be and can deliver more than just education.** While the alternative schools created to address the special needs of the disaffected and disadvantaged are specifically designed to be "nonschool-like" both in structure and operation, even Sweden's conventional upper secondary schools are unconventional by U.S. standards—mixing the world of academics and the world of work, and even changing the venue for education from school to factory to underscore the relationship between the two. What's more, Sweden uses its schools, especially its alternative schools, as central points of access for a variety of services needed by the disadvantaged or disaffected young people they serve—providing not just education, but job training, work experience, health services, welfare services, and individual and family counseling. The approach is holistic, aimed at strengthening the entire individual at once.

4. **Teachers—especially nonconformist teachers—can be the driving forces of educational innovation.** Virtually every alternative education and training program underway in Gothenburg was the creation of one or more teachers who were themselves disaffected by the regimentation of the school system and its inability to reach some segments of the school-age population. Their success underscores a basic principle: that teacher-centered solutions work.

5. **The central challenge in reaching all young people, but particularly the disadvantaged or disaffected, is "empowerment"—providing them opportunities to choose their own futures, to take ownership of their own solutions.** The Swedes have enormous faith in individuals and in their ability to make the right choices for themselves, given good information and flexible programs. Despite their socialist image, their programs are highly individualized.

# CHAPTER 3

# WEST GERMANY:
# The Credentialed Society

*The "Help Wanted" signs are up all over Bavaria. In booming Munich, the sleek high-fashion shops on Maximilianstrasse are short of clerks. The windows of the employment service on busy Sonnenstrasse are packed with job vacancy notices. West of the city, near the site of the 1972 Olympics, a gleaming high-tech auto mechanics training school is filled to capacity with earnest young apprentices. Still, Bernd Klingsohr, owner of a major BMW dealership in Munich, complains he needs more skilled workers. In fact, in Upper Bavaria alone, there are 30,000 more vacancies than there are apprentices to fill them.*

*Throughout Germany, industry is producing at nearly 90 percent of capacity and the Chancellor's office has had to revise growth projections upward repeatedly. Bavaria's economy, growing faster than any other German state, is as robustly healthy as the waitresses who bustle through Munich's Augustinerkeller beer garden bearing as many as eight quarts of beer with little apparent effort. And yet the German economy also bears a heavy burden: in the midst of the most prosperous period in recent memory, the national unemployment rate hovers stubbornly around 8.6 percent. Like most Western industrial nations, most of Germany's unemployment is structural—concentrated in older heavy industries located predominantly in the north and affecting, for the most part, low- or narrowly-skilled workers.*

*Unlike other Western nations, however, young people do not comprise a significant portion of the unemployed population in Germany. In fact, Germany has the lowest level of youth unemployment in Europe. The reason is "The Dual System"— the current incarnation of Germany's centuries-old tradition of apprenticeship and vocational training. Financed and operated jointly by private businesses and the state, and covering virtually every occupation imaginable, the dual system produces for the German economy a steady stream of highly qualified workers* whose credentials are recognized and respected throughout the nation—and throughout Europe as well.

Nevertheless, Hans Baumgartler, Director of the Electrical Guild of Munich, is worried. Seated in his glass-enclosed conference room on a rooftop high above downtown Munich, Herr Baumgartler is worried about the coming invasion: a potential flood of competitors from France—and elsewhere in Europe—when the EC integrates its goods and services markets in 1992. The craftsman in him leads Herr Baumgartler to worry about the lowering of standards caused by competitors who will not have Journeyman and Master certification. The businessman in him worries that, not having had to bear the cost of obtaining such credentials, these competitors will undercut German companies.

Others in Munich, and elsewhere in Germany, are worried too—not about the skill levels of workers from elsewhere, but about the skill levels of Germany's own workers. There is little question that Germany has a superbly qualified workforce, but some suggest that the dual system has produced workers whose skills are so narrow that they may be unable to adapt to change—and thus be rendered uncompetitive despite their skills.

As a result, as it has for centuries, Germany's vocational education system is changing—seeking to produce workers who can think as well as use their hands—and thus retain Germany's reputation for creating perhaps the world's top technicians.

## Public Education in Germany: A Place for Everyone, and Everyone in His Place

The Bavarian Constitution requires that the state provide an educational system for all children "according to their intelligence, interests, and abilities." Thus, we are forced to have a differentiated system; we cannot have a uniform or comprehensive system as there is in the United States. It would be unconstitutional.

—Karl-Heinz Freund, Bavarian Ministry of Education

The West German public educational system is complex and strictly segmented. Primary school begins at age 7 and ends at age 10, at which time school officials, using students' average grades and teachers' recommendations, send children on to one of two (and in some states three) kinds of secondary school. Most go on to the main secondary school (Hauptschule) which prepares young people for trade apprenticeships. A smaller number go on to grammar school (Gymnasium) and pursue a classical education, generally leading to university.

But this decision is not final. In a nation which places great weight on formal professional credentials, there is a great deal of social pressure for children to attend grammar school, despite the range of alternatives. In part as a consequence, therefore, there are "bridges" to the Gymnasium provided at several points in a child's educational career. For example, parents may appeal an elementary school's recommendation immediately and have their children placed in grammar school "on probation" for several days at the beginning of the next school year and then await a further, final decision by school officials. Alternatively, students sent to main secondary school at age 10 may, at age 12, take an examination to advance to either grammar school or a third "intermediate secondary school" (Realschule) which combines both academic and vocational coursework. (In some German states, Realschule is a third option when the first "cut" occurs at age 10.)

The length of secondary school education depends upon the type of school a student attends. Students attending Gymnasium, which is more academically rigorous than American high schools, continue until age 19, then take a final examination for entry to university. Intermediate secondary school (Realschule) students complete school at age 16 to 17 and may take another "bridge" to grammar school for a few more years and then take the exam for university, or go directly to one of several higher technical-vocation schools and colleges, or enter an apprenticeship. But most young people—those attending the main secondary school (Hauptschule)—complete their compulsory education at age 15 to 16 at the end of 9th grade and pursue an apprenticeship in a specific trade.

## The "Dual System": Germany's National Skill-Building Partnership

*Who is a master? He who has invented
something. Who is a journeyman? He who has
acquired skills. Who is an apprentice? Everyone.*

—Johann Wolfgang v. Goethe

*"Theory" is when you know how something works,
but it doesn't. "Practice" is when something
works, but you don't know why.*

—Sign in an automotive mechanics
training school in Munich

The process of assuring a skilled workforce is more formalized in West Germany than in any other Western nation—and has been for centuries. Since the Middle Ages, craft guilds have relied upon a rigorous apprenticeship system to produce generation after generation of highly skilled craftsmen. Until the mid-1800s, this system was solely the responsibility of private employers. But by 1869, in part to assure uniform standards of quality, a national industrial code provided that manufacturers could be required to send their apprentices to a "continuation school" for further education and training. Thus was born the "dual system"—a partnership of government and private industry to produce workers skilled in both the theory and practice of their trade, learned on the job and in vocational school and supplemented occasionally by courses in specialized training centers. By 1912, when the present system of vocational schools was established, the government's role was strengthened and in 1938 part-time attendance in vocational schools was made a mandatory component of every apprenticeship.

Today, fully two-thirds of all secondary school graduates enter the dual system. Most will have been introduced to the world of work during "Arbeitslehrer"—a formal learning program about industry that began in 1953 and is part of the compulsory school curriculum in all schools except Gymnasium. Compulsory school graduates choose among some 480 different trades and, at the age of 15 or 16, seek an employer willing to take them on as an apprentice. The employer and would-be employee enter into a written contract which stipulates the responsibilities of each and confirms how much the apprentice will be paid, based on a minimum level negotiated nationally between unions and employer associations.

For most trades, the apprenticeship lasts three years, during which time the apprentice spends an average of four days each week on the job working under the guidance of a Master or an approved instructor, and one day a week at a local state-run vocational school (Berufschule) specializing in that trade. The job of the vocational school is to ensure uniform and consistent theoretical training and to compensate for differences in learning experiences from one company to another.

The operational mechanics aside, the heart of the dual system is the relationship between trainee and employer. It operates as a kind of national mentoring program, with young people from a wide range of backgrounds learning and maturing under the guidance of a demanding but caring master. The emphasis on skill-building and craftsmanship makes apprenticeships a transforming experience—one that builds confidence and self-esteem as carefully as it builds practical skills. Not only does this help assure better craft workers, but it also creates a pool from which many of the nation's middle managers are drawn.

At the conclusion of the three years, after passing both a nationally-administered written examination and a practical examination, the apprentice becomes a journeyman, whose credentials will be recognized and accepted anywhere in Germany he or she seeks work. After working for at least three more years, and attending additional courses in business management, law, and technology, a journeyman may take an examination to become a master. No craftsman can open a business in Germany without becoming a master first.

### Skill Depth: Industry's Role

*Bernd Klingsohr, owner of one of Munich's largest BMW dealerships, is shocked to learn that many Americans mistrust their auto mechanics and even more astonished to learn that there is no officially-sanctioned universal system of assuring the credentials of people who repair cars. His service department employs six masters and 21 journeymen. In addition, he has 15 apprentices—five each in their first, second, and third years of training. Anything less than exceptional service is, for him, simply unthinkable. He adds, however, that maintaining this dependable level of quality is costly. In addition to the more than 15,000 DM he pays his apprentices each year, the dealership maintains a classroom filled with video training equipment (produced by BMW) and monthly technical workbooks (produced by the automotive trade association under the guidance of the Ministry of Economics). The master mechanics on the staff spend part of their time teaching the apprentices in this classroom.*

*Yet it is clear that Herr Klingsohr is of two minds on the subject of the dual system. On the one hand, he is intensely proud of the quality of the specialists he produces, of the relationship he has with his young apprentices, and of the reputation that his business has gained. On the other hand, he is bedeviled by major auto manufacturing companies, including BMW, who wait for him to train journeymen and then lure them away, rather than training their own. And he is frustrated by the unfairness of the fact that the government will pay for the education of university students, to the tune of some 100,000 DM each, while leaving the bulk of the cost of apprenticeship training up to private industry. Still, he says, he has no choice: if the country is to have a competitive workforce and maintain its international reputation for precision and quality, the dual system must be supported. What's more, his customers demand it. "He will not prosper, unless he trains," he says. And the frustration in his voice a moment earlier is replaced, once again, by pride.*

All businesses in Germany must, by law, be members of either the Chamber of Trade and Craft or the Chamber of Industry and Commerce (many are members of both). The chambers are private organizations funded largely by the member companies. The chambers, which represent both employers and employees, have a number of functions, among which include advising the state on apprenticeship and vocational education standards, supervising apprenticeship training, and operating vocational training centers on behalf of the state in places where state vocational schools do not exist.

One level down in the private sector institutional hierarchy, trade guilds, also funded by member companies, operate specialized technical training centers on behalf of their members. As part of their on-the-job training, apprentices (as well as journeymen seeking their master certification) attend courses at these guild centers to have the opportunity to learn the latest technology and work on the most advanced equipment—supplementing what they are able to learn at the shops where they are apprenticing and at the state Berufschule.

Finally, individual private businesses are the foundation of the dual system. Not all businesses participate and most of the ones that do are, somewhat surprisingly, small. Some 50 percent of the companies in the Chamber of Trade and Craft (which tends to represent smaller companies with an average of 8 employees) offer apprenticeships, but only 25 percent of the members of the Chamber of Industry and Commerce (which tends to represent larger industries) offer them. Though supervised by the chambers, businesses are given wide latitude as to how they will run their apprenticeship programs. Still, a business owner taking on an apprentice shoulders a significant burden. First, the salary, though small, will be much higher than the young employee is worth; it will be years before the apprentice's work brings in any appreciable income. Second, the owner, or one of his master technicians, will generate less income than he or she might otherwise because of the time devoted to training. Third, the owner bears the additional cost of providing special training materials for the apprentices. Fourth, in addition to paying his membership to both the chamber and his respective guild, he will be expected to pay the apprentice's tuition for guild-run special training courses. Finally, having made this investment, the owner runs the risk of having his apprentice lured away by a larger company when the apprentice becomes a journeyman.

Despite these costs and risks, the dual system thrives. There are more than 600,000 apprenticeships in Germany nationwide, and more than 35,000 in Upper Bavaria alone. It thrives, if Munich business owners are any measure, simply because people believe in it and are convinced that it is the only way to ensure a steady supply of skilled workers with reliable credentials.

### Skill Breadth: Government's Role

*The state vocational school on Munich's west side that Martin Deschermeier heads is, at least at first glance, a far cry from the sparkling training centers run by Bavaria's guilds. An old building, it has the down-at-the heels scruffiness common to turn-of-the- century public school buildings everywhere: dingy rooms with high ceilings, daylight filtered through windows coated with decades of chalk dust, institutional green halls, scuffed linoleum.*

*But in the training labs the scene is different. Among the state-of-the-art machines that pack its labs, Munich's automotive technology vocational school has a brand new, 12-cylinder BMW 750i, broken down into its component systems, for students to work on. Perhaps the most technically advanced car in the world, it would retail at nearly $70,000 in the United States. Yet less than nine months since its commercial introduction, the car has been donated by the manufacturer.*

The vocational schools that constitute the government half of the dual system—the schools apprentices must attend an average of one day each week (or the equivalent in "block courses" that may run for an entire week or more)—are run independently by each German state under federal guidelines and using curricula developed jointly with industry. The buildings, instructors, teaching materials, and most testing equipment are paid for by taxpayers. Tuition is free. However, as in Herr Deschermeier's auto technology school—one of 13 vocational schools in Munich, each covering a different field—all the products students work on typically are donated by the manufacturers.

Public vocational education is a crucial part of the dual system—the part that ensures that any journeyman from any part of Germany can be relied upon to possess thorough knowledge of his trade regardless of where he took his apprenticeship. It is the essential element which assures that credentials can be depended upon to signify skill. Given the differences from one apprentice shop to another, the mandatory attendance at vocational school must be given a good deal of the credit for Germany's reputation for consistently high quality workmanship.

The vocational school is also designed to make the transition from school to work smoother both for the student and for the potential employer. With the recent addition of the Basic Vocational Year, the schools give students more time to learn about the specific trades within broad fields before they commit themselves to an apprenticeship. Before choosing to become a baker, for example, a student will be exposed to a wide range of trades in the food preparation field. This year accomplishes two goals: it helps insure that young people will be happy with the choice they make (and provides opportunities for would-be apprentices, and potential employers to evaluate each other); and it helps ensure that their basic skills will broaden beyond the trade they pursue, increasing their value to their employers.

## Cracks in the Monolith: Challenges Facing the Dual System

The dual system has not survived for more than a century without adapting to changing circumstances. And today, it faces significant new pressures—from both inside and outside the system.

### Breadth vs. Depth: The Content Challenge

The extremely low level of youth unemployment in West Germany attests to the success of the dual system in overcoming the problem that bedevils the United States—school leavers who are not work-ready. Sweden's solution to this problem is to provide a significant amount of work-related training while young people are still in school. West Germany's solution is to introduce the world of work during "Arbeitslehrer," but then let employers bear most of the formal training burden, with the vocational education system helping out.

But as the pace of technological change accelerates and the need for a range of general skills begins to rival the need for specific skills, German educators and labor market specialists are suggesting that the one day per week of vocational school is not enough. They argue that the only way to assure that the nation's future workforce will have broad enough skills to continue to compete internationally is to emphasize on-the-job training less and emphasize basic education and broad vocational training more—specifically by increasing the vocational school attendance requirement for apprentices from one day per week to two. Not surprisingly, employers—who bear most of the financial costs of the dual system—are not pleased with the prospect of apprentices who may contribute even less to the productivity of their businesses than they do now. Nor are they pleased with the prospect of more government control of the content of apprenticeship training.

But broadening the base of apprentice training may not be enough, in part because the narrowing effect of specialization does not stop there. The process of apprenticeship-journeyman-master certification, spread over a decade of work experience and training at minimum, appears to have the effect of deepening and solidifying skill specialization, rather than broadening it. As a consequence, the German labor force has a dual reputation, of both high skill and high inflexibility.

## Substandard Compulsory School Graduates: The Raw Materials Challenge

Employers and vocational education officials complain that the quality of the raw material inputs to the dual system—secondary school graduates—is declining. Bernhard Huser, director of the glittering new guild-run automobile technology training center near Munich's Olympic Park, confesses that there is little that the employer side of the dual system can do for such young people; employers simply do not have the capability to provide remedial programs. Whether this decline is real or only perceived is hard to determine. Certainly the number of jobs available for low-skilled, inadequately educated workers in Germany is declining, as it is in other industrialized nations. The general increase in the education and skill requirements of most new jobs may simply make new entrants to the workforce appear poorly prepared—in short, demand may be affecting perceptions about supply.

To an extent, providing further education in language and math is one of the reasons that the Basic Vocational Year was recently introduced in the Berufschule curriculum. In addition, the Department of Labor runs pre-apprenticeship preparation programs. But no one claims that postsecondary remedial programs are an adequate solution.

Education specialists cite the usual litany of causes for the perceived decline in the quality of Hauptschule graduates: too much leisure time, too much money, welfare dependency, single-parent families, and so forth. But vocational counselors suggest something more fundamental in the culture of education in Germany. They argue that the pressure—created by parents and society in general—

for young people to gain entry to the prestigous and highly-competitive grammar school system has a debilitating effect on the majority of young people who are not accepted. Branded as "failures" at age 10, they have low expectations and little motivation to excel in Hauptschule. It is left to the dual system to help them catch up. But the dual system—which assumes basic levels of education and motivation in would-be apprentices—was not designed as a remedial education system. As with the breadth vs. depth issue, the solution seems to be more time in school and less on the job—a prospect not relished by the nation's employers.

## Minorities and Women: The Opportunity Challenge

Of the nearly 60 million people in West Germany, nearly 5 million are foreign nationals, many of them "guest workers" invited from lesser developed countries to work in German factories during a period of labor shortage more than two decades ago. Though their labor was largely unskilled and their earnings relatively low, many stayed on, working and raising families in Germany while preserving their own cultural identities.

While it forbids these workers, or their children, from becoming citizens, Germany has worked hard to provide them with mainstream educational opportunities and integrate them into the dual system. It has not been easy. Language proficiency has been the principal barrier, one that is complicated by Germany's commitment to teaching guest workers' children in their native language (in some states even in their own schools) so as to preserve their cultural identity.

In the early 1980's, a period of labor surplus, more journeymen were coming out of the dual system than there was demand for their skills. Many of these skilled workers took unskilled jobs in factories, in the process squeezing out the less skilled guest workers. Because of that experience, and the general decline in the availability of unskilled work in general, many guest workers have pursued apprenticeships—especially service professions like barbers and hairdressers—with the encouragement of the government. However, even in the current period of labor shortage, there is a distinct—if largely unvocalized—resentment that foreign nationals are taking jobs from German nationals. Should the booming German economy begin to slow, this problem may grow.

A similar problem exists for women. Despite special efforts to encourage young women to enter nontraditional fields, West Germany's vocational education system, like Sweden's, remains heavily skewed by gender. Of the roughly 4,000 apprentices in Herr Deschermeier's auto, machine, and aircraft technology school in Munich, for example, only 65 are women. According to vocational specialists, the resistance stems both from the demand side and from the supply side. While many employers in traditionally male trades continue to shun women apprentices, some employers are willing, even eager to hire women (though they have not been as eager during periods of labor surplus). They claim, however, that young German women simply resist nontraditional occupations.

## 1992: The Zeitgeist Challenge

The imminent 1992 integration of goods and services markets among EC countries poses a clear threat to the dual system and to German businesses. The small businesses that typically are members of the Chamber of Trade and Craft are especially concerned about the potential flood of uncertified competitor companies run by foreign owners who lack master credentials and staffed by workers who lack journeyman credentials. German business owners fear they will be squeezed out by cut-rate competitors who do not bear the burden of the costs associated with acquiring such credentials. (Ironically, other European nations fear the sudden invasion of German competitors, with their international reputation for quality.)

But there is a deeper fear that goes beyond business competition. It is the fear that 1992 will undermine the cultural foundations of the dual system and, worse, Germany's long tradition of dependably high levels of competence—undermine, in effect, what it means to be a German craftsman.

## Lessons from the German Dual System

Over the centuries, the dual system and its predecessors have proved to be highly adaptable in the face of changing conditions. Despite the challenges on the horizon, the dual system is so deeply ingrained in the German economy and in German cultural tradition that it is likely not just to survive, but to thrive. It emphasizes many of the characteristics the emerging economy requires of the workforce: on-the-spot, pragmatic problem-solving and flexibility among many tasks. Other nations are struggling to replicate it. The bottom line is that, whatever its flaws or uncertainties, the dual system is unquestionably successful at minimizing youth unemployment and producing skilled workers. Under the circumstances, there are several lessons to consider:

1. **Credentials Count.** As markets become more integrated, not just in Europe but internationally, the issue of workforce credentials takes on increased significance. Credentials serve as de facto seals of quality—guarantees of dependable levels of competence. Although German business owners worry about the erosion of the dual system after 1992, in fact the EC is working on developing a similar concept, calling it the "Alternative System." Perhaps more importantly, the formalized credential-building that lies at the core of the dual system is the source of Germany's low youth unemployment levels and stands in stark contrast to America's "Forgotten Half" problem—the low incomes and limited economic prospects of those who do not attend college. Today, persuading American employers to hire disadvantaged individuals who have completed any of the hundreds of training courses in the haphazard system of government-assisted job training currently in place is an uphill battle. Not surprisingly, they avoid what they perceive to be "damaged goods" and seek known commodities. As a consequence, college degrees have become requirements for thousands of jobs that, in fact, require far less formal education. A universally recognized, noncollege credential-building system would provide the kind of assurance employers seek and customers demand.

2. **Basic education levels are a prerequisite of training.** Certain basic levels of competence in reading, calculating, and problem solving are fundamental requirements for effective vocational training. If the secondary school system cannot guarantee that school-leavers will possess these capabilities, post-secondary training programs will have no choice but to develop alternatives. Indeed, given the speed with which skill demands are changing, any training system—whether for young people or adults—may have to assume some level of remedial work.

3. **Employer participation and financial commitment is crucial.** Employers are the players who know best what kinds of skills are needed in the workplace. They are also the principal beneficiaries of training programs. Thus, they should have major—though not exclusive—responsibility for the design, execution, and financing of vocational training programs. In this, Sweden and Germany agree, though they differ on where the training is delivered—Sweden delivering vocational training intensively in the classroom before young people leave school, Germany delivering it principally on the job. Differences in size and sophistication among shops can be corrected by pooling resources, as the guild training centers do. The German labor unions, which support the dual system in almost all its particulars, argue that financing should change—though still be borne largely by employers. The unions argue that if all companies were required to contribute to a national training fund, more employers would find it in their interest to provide apprenticeships, and quality—which would be overseen by the fund—would be more uniform. Nevertheless, the unions and the employers are united in commitment to the notion that employers should be in the lead, not government. This solidarity of purpose contrasts sharply with the British approach (see chapter on Great Britain) and with most training programs for young people and the disadvantaged in the United States.

4. **Partnerships work.** Both the Swedish system and the German dual system rest on a firm foundation of employer-union-government cooperation. Each player has a part. The shared responsibility acts in the same way as the American system of checks and balances. There is a kind of viscerally universal agreement on the objective, backed by negotiated agreements on the process and how the bill is to be split. Such explicit national tripartite arrangements may translate less well in the United States than the central notion of widely shared consensus on these issues.

5. **Any school-to-work transition system must include investment by the individuals being trained.** In both the in-school training system in Sweden and the on-the-job apprenticeship in Germany, the young trainee receives an in-

come. But the income is modest, not a living wage, and both systems require a personal commitment of at least three years of study and training at that income level. In short, each system requires individuals to invest in their own futures—to defer the higher present income they might receive from a low-skill factory job for the deferred rewards of a higher-skilled, and higher-paying, job in the future.

6. **In capitalist economies, work guarantees are equivocal.** The dual system works brilliantly in a growing economy, but less well in recessions. If there are more young people seeking apprenticeships than there are places for them, youth unemployment will grow. If they find places but the economy fails to produce jobs for them once they have become journeymen, then they will feel betrayed. Unlike Sweden, there is no work guarantee built into Germany's dual system—though the master-apprentice relationship may increase the chances of being kept on in tight times.

7. **"Streaming"—separating children by performance levels at an early age—may create more problems than it solves.** Segregating young students by perceived levels of ability creates difficult educational, social, and economic problems later on. Students told repeatedly from an early age that they do not measure up sooner or later will come to believe it and their levels of commitment and effort will decline. The process is self-fulfilling. Furthermore, social pressure works against any school other than the most esteemed. Similar but less overt systems in the United States have the same effect. There is a special irony that in Germany, with a wide array of choices in educational opportunity, social pressure to follow only the grammar school route is enormous. Students who become defeatist in school will prove poorly motivated when they leave school. While Germany is experimenting with schools for students with mixed abilities, streaming remains a fundamental, and problematic, element of the public school system and one that places extra burdens on the dual system.

# CHAPTER 4

# FRANCE:
# A Nation Decentralizes

*On the outskirts of the beautiful French city of Amiens—indeed, on the outskirts of French society—sits Amiens Nord, a "new town" of some 18,000 people. It is a brutally sterile place. Rows of ten-story-high, hundred-yard-long cement high-rise apartment buildings sit—massive, silent, and monumental—like giant headstones on the bare ground.*

*Separated from the rest of Amiens by a high-speed, multi-lane divided highway as effectively as if by a moat, Amiens Nord has none of the local amenities common to a living community—no grocery stores, no drugstores, no cleaners, no cafes or newstands. Residents call the flat, unlandscaped spaces between the buildings "no-man's-land." The people of Amiens Nord, principally first- and second-generation immigrants from some 26 different countries, are as socially and economically isolated from mainstream Amiens as they are physically isolated. There are no businesses in Amiens Nord, and there are no jobs. Unemployment is three times the average for Amiens in general, and among the highest in France. This is particularly true for young people, who represent 50 percent of the population. Partly as a consequence, vandalism, crime, and delinquency have been high.*

*In the midst of this bleak landscape, however, there are signs of important changes underway. In several places, the facades of the buildings are being improved. Inside, apartments are being renovated. New and, in some cases, quite stunningly designed entranceways are being built. Small parks and vegetable gardens have been incorporated into the site and a new youth center has been designed and built by young people from the housing projects.*

*Less visible, but more important in the long run, youth training and adult literacy programs have been established. Day-care, child care, and health services are increasingly available; programs which celebrate, rather than sublimate, the cultural diversity of the community have been established; and fairs, a newspaper, and even radio and closed-circuit television news and community events programs have been developed for residents in the project.*

*Amiens Nord is emblematic of a revolution underway in France—a radical restructuring of how French government operates and how public services, from housing to training, from delinquency prevention to health services, are delivered to disadvantaged segments of the population. The problems the French face are not novel, but some of their solutions are.*

## France Responds to Communities in Crisis

*"Our housing crisis coincided with a crisis in architecture and city planning."*

—Bernard Meyer
Local Planning Official, Amiens, France

In the summer of 1981, a wave of riots and arson flashed through the suburbs of several French cities and brought French officials face to face with the acute social and economic deprivation of hundreds of thousands of French and immigrant families living in the nation's huge public housing projects.

The violence was probably inevitable. What was surprising was that it had not happened sooner.

Between 1950 and the mid-1970s, the demographics of France underwent a dramatic shift. Thousands of poor, rural French families moved from the provinces to the cities to seek work, rapidly swelling urban populations. They were joined by equally large numbers of immigrants who moved to France to work in its growing automobile and construction industries.

To cope with the sudden housing crisis, the French rushed to complete hundreds of massive public housing projects. Poorly designed, poorly constructed, and poorly maintained, the projects became breeding grounds for social discontent. Isolated from the communities to which they were attached, and populated by marginally-educated and poorly-skilled families who were hard-hit when the economy turned sluggish in the late 1970s, the projects deteriorated—the deterioration accelerated by inadequate public investments in maintenance and basic public services.

When violence erupted in 1981, France responded uncharacteristically. Long one of the most centralized governments in Europe—and one in which public agencies interacted infrequently—the French concluded that the social and educational problems that led to the violence were so complex that only cross-cutting and locally-delivered solutions would work. In fact, the recommendation for locally-based solutions made by the organization created to address the housing project crisis, the National Commission for the Redevelopment of Public Housing Districts, echoed developments elsewhere in French government. At roughly the same time, two other closely-related initiatives were being developed to improve economic conditions in France's most disadvantaged neighborhoods and, in particular, to help disadvantaged young people. They were the National Council for Delinquency Prevention and the "Missions Locales" initiative of the Delegation for Youth in Difficulty.

Together, these three initiatives, underway now for several years, consitute nothing less than a revolution in French governance—a dramatic shift from a highly centralized, bureaucratic system to one which is localized, based upon public/private partnerships, intergovernmental, and highly entrepreneurial.

## *National Commission for the Redevelopment of Public Housing Districts: Local Solutions to a National Crisis*

If anything, the National Commission is misnamed. A national body does exist, on which are represented some 11 ministries, as well as labor unions, and residents' associations, among others. But while this body establishes the main policy guidelines and passes them through regional commissions, the principal operational component is the local commission, chaired by a mayor, staffed by an executive director, and composed of representatives of housing authorities and residents' associations, social workers and local organizers, and local deliverers of public social programs (health, welfare, education, training, etc.).

In 1982, the National Commission defined four essential principles for the redevelopment of disadvantaged communities:

- Solutions must be comprehensive—going beyond renovation of housing to include other causes of urban decline—education, job training, economic development, culture, health, recreation, among others;

- They must be decentralized—designed and managed by local government, from conception to implementation;
- There must be broad citizen involvement—so that residents and community groups can create their own futures, with assistance from government; and
- State social services (including financial support must be integrated and coordinated at the local level.

The embodiment of these principles is a detailed, formal contract—developed by local commissions and submitted to the regional and national commissions. The contract specifies the local government's objectives, budget and financing plan, implementation program, and organizational structure, and serves as the vehicle for funding support and service delivery by national social service agencies.

Beginning with 22 sites in 1982, the program grew to 150 sites by 1987. It was incorporated into the 1984-1988 national Five Year Plan for economic development and will be included (in part because of the uniformly strong support of mayors) in the 1989-1993 Five Year Plan as well. The national government funds only about a third of the total cost of the projects currently underway. Another roughly 22 percent of the funding comes from the regional councils, and the balance is funded by local government and their private sector partners. National government commitments have averaged approximately 500 million francs per year for housing rehabilitation and 190 million francs per year for community development projects (social, cultural, recreational, economic, etc.).

By far the greatest accomplishments have been in the rehabilitation of the housing projects themselves. Many have become attractive, efficient, and safe places for people to live. Perhaps more important have been the community development projects—day care and child care, cultural programs, job training and delinquency prevention (see program descriptions below), and the like.

Efforts to make France's rigidly hierarchical school system an active member of the local teams have been less successful. Adversarial relationships exist between parents and school officials, between the teachers' union and school officials, and between school officials and local governments. The concept of teachers providing additional help for disadvantaged students, for example, is a novel one and, at least until recently, dropouts were prohibited from returning to school.

Still, the locally planned, locally run program is a fundamental departure from tradition in France and has had exceptional success throughout the nation. As it has matured, the program has become increasingly experimental, with local officials creating highly entrepreneurial variations of the main theme.

## *"Mission Locales":*
## *Smoothing the School-to-Work Transition*

The willingness of the French to seek out and grapple with the root causes of social and economic problems, rather than simply addressing the most obvious or pressing symptoms, is further illustrated by the "Missions Locales" (local task force) program for helping young people make the transition from school to work.

In February 1982, at the same time that the public housing project initiative was begun, the French government created an experimental system of local task forces aimed at addressing youth employment problems. The initiative was the result of 1981 report to the government which concluded that the integration of young people into the mainstream of the nation's economy should be a top priority of government.

At the core of the Missions Locales program is the integrated delivery, at a single point in local communities, of a wide range of social, economic, and educational services currently offered by a number of public and private agencies, including job training, work experience programs, adult literacy programs, health and welfare services, housing and transportation assistance, and individual or family counseling. There is even an experimental program underway in 38 Missions Locales to identify the new skill demands associated with technological change—a program operated in conjunction with 125 commercial and industrial firms and 75 agricultural firms and involving some 500 young people. The "one-stop-shop" approach is designed both to improve the efficiency of the delivery of these services and, perhaps more important, to make them more easily accessible to the young people who need them most—those who are poorly educated or lack job skills—when and where they need them. In contrast to the standard view of the centralized, segmented, bureaucratic nature of French government, the Missions Locales are decidedly unbureaucratic.

The purposes of the Missions Locales program are:

- to contact, provide guidance and assistance to, and follow up with youth (age 16–25) "in difficulty";
- to establish, or take better advantage of, local job training and education programs for young people;
- to generate new jobs and other creative activities for young people; and
- to improve the personal and social conditions of the  target population.

The operational heart of a Mission Locale is a team of 10 or 12 professionals, some appointed by the local governing board and others made available by social service agencies. The program is headed by an executive director and typically operates out of an easy-to-find local office or storefront (though in rural areas they may only be open part-time). The governing board—composed of local elected officials, employment and job training services, educators, cultural and recreational authorities, employers, unions, chambers of commerce, and associations—sets priorities and supervises the program. Financing is provided both by the national government and by local government. The projected 1988 Missions Locales budget, for example, is 130 million francs, of which slightly more than half (70 million francs) will be provided by local government, both as cash and as in-kind services (staff, offices, etc.).

There were 53 Missions Locales established initially in 1983 and a little more than 120 in 1987. In 1988, 50 more were proposed to be created. In 1987, roughly 170,000 of the nation's estimated 400,000 youth "in difficulty" were participating actively in Missions Locales around the country. Of this total, roughly 10 percent have graduated from high school, but are functionally illiterate; 70 percent have graduated with substandard diplomas or have no diploma at all; and the balance are individuals with drug, alcohol, or other personal problems. Participation by young people entails no special obligations, involves very little paperwork, and is purely voluntary.

Where possible, Missions Locales operate jointly with the public housing project programs—as is the case in Amiens Nord. Some 50 of the 100 Missions Locales in urban areas work closely with housing project programs. The balance of the Missions Locales are in rural areas or small towns.

To improve the transition from school to work for their clients, the Missions Locales serve as local agents for three programs:

1. **Public/Community Works Projects** (with the acronym "TUC" in French)—in which six-month to one-year internships are available for young people 16-25 years of age, involving four hours per day of work and four of training. A wage of 1,259 francs per month is paid by the state, to which an additional 500 francs are added by the employer. This is less than the minimum wage, but the program does provide meaningful professional training.

2. **Internships in Private Companies** (with the French acronym "SVIP")—in which young people work full time for 3 to 6 months and receive training one week per month. Their wages (more than in the TUC) are paid by a foundation jointly funded by companies and labor unions, but Social Security is paid by the state.

3. **Professional Job Training**—in which the Missions Locales develop for each individual a "training itinerary" designed both to enhance their skills and provide them enough work to solve their short-term income needs. The itineraries are a kind of "moral contract" between the individual and the program.

Carefully targeted to the needs of their clients and locally focused, the Missions Locales have grown rapidly in the past five years and enjoy the support of both socialist and conservative political parties in France. Moreover, they have begun to increase public recognition that France's public school system is failing to meet the education and skill needs of a significant number of its students—and failing to produce sufficient technically-trained young people to meet the needs of an increasingly technological economy.

But the most important lesson of the Missions Locales is that comprehensive, integrated educational, training, and social services, locally delivered and sensitive to local needs, can improve the transition for disadvantaged young people from school to the working world.

### *The National Council for Delinquency Prevention: Communities Take Ownership of the Behavior of Their Children*

*"We want everyone in our community to feel they have responsibility for solving delinquency and other youth-related problems."*

—Local Government Representative,
National Council on Delinquency Prevention

Successive waves of violence and delinquency among young people in the mid-1970s and early 1980s, and at least three major national studies to address the problem, led to the creation in June 1983 of a National Council for Delinquency Prevention. The Council—chaired by the Prime Minister and including members from the Assembly and Senate, mayors of 35 cities, the representatives of 28 associations and, as ex officio members, the ministers of Interior, Public Safety, Justice, Social Welfare, Defense, Economy and Finance, Education, Culture, Immigrants, Youth and Sport, Urban Development, Housing, and Training—was charged with the responsibility for:

- Developing and maintaining information on the nature and extent of the delinquency problem;
- Recommending to public authorities measures to prevent it;
- Increasing public understanding of these problems;
- Carrying out studies and research;
- Producing and publishing annual reports on delinquency prevention; and
- Overseeing the creation and operation of local delinquency prevention organizations.

This last purpose—the creation of local delinquency prevention organizations—is the third significant locally-managed youth transition program of major importance in France.

As with the "Missions Locales," the heart of France's delinquency prevention program is a locally created and operated organization explicitly designed to create local ownership of both the problem of youth crime and of solutions to it. Technically, a regional (state) council oversees the work of the local organizations, but the bulk of the responsibility lies with local governments.

As with the public housing program, the central feature of the delinquency prevention program is a formal, signed contract between the local council and the national government. The contract is a comprehensive document, covering dropout prevention, dropout assistance programs, vocational training and job search assistance, young adult literacy programs, a wide variety of recreational and sport programs, housing assistance, drug prevention, and special programs for the summer, among others. A section on "justice" deals with conciliation and mediation programs; housing, education and training for newly released prisoners; and help for victims of crime.

The focus of the program is not so much on direct action as it is on coordinating other social services at the local level and communicating the causes of delinquency and youth violence within the community. The coordinating and largely voluntary nature of the program is reflected in the budget. In fiscal 1988, the total national and local budget for the program, which currently operates in 527 towns (up from 18 in 1983) will be only 50 million francs.

### The Workforce Connection: The High Committee on Education and Industry Relations

*"We have rehabilitated the buildings, but not the people who live in them."*

—Local Planning Official from Amiens, France

The root of the "Youth In Difficulty" problem in France is a school system that produces graduates who are poorly prepared for the world of work and an economy that does not create enough work for those who are prepared. The lack of active involvement of the school system and the absence of significant economic growth and enterprise development initiatives at the local level suggest that programs like those underway in Amiens Nord may be little more than holding actions. That is, they keep young people off the streets, but do little to change their prospects.

The High Committee on Education and Industry Relations, established in 1985 by the Minister of Education, may help address these deeper issues. As a start, the Committee involves the industrial world for the first time in defining and helping to implement proposals for France's education and training system. In 1987, the Committee released a report calling for a number of changes in the relationships between schools and industry, including local school-industry "twinning" (something like compacts); updating the qualifications for graduation from compulsory school; increasing the number of young people attaining the "Baccalaureate" degree level from 150,000 to 250,000 per year; increasing the number of young people seeking higher, post-"Bac" technical qualifications from 80,000 to 160,000 per year; and strengthening engineering training.

It remains to be seen whether these recommendations will be translated into concrete improvements in the French school system's ability to produce work-ready workers for the French economy. With the workforce competitiveness challenge of the integration of the Common Market only a few years away, France's school system, and the workers it has produced, have a lot of catching up to do.

## Lessons from France

After centuries of centralization—of all power being vested in Paris and all public policy emanating from Paris—France is gradually reinventing itself, shifting the locus of social action to local government and devising an innovative array of partnerships for helping disadvantaged communities and young people and smoothing the school-to-work transition. In part because policymaking was massively centralized for so long, experimentation is widespread today. Several lessons arise from these experiments:

1. **Locally based solutions are preferable to national programs.** No national program can hope to accommodate the intricacies of local situations; localities must own their own problems and craft their own solutions. The result is not just

more sensitive local programs, but a much wider universe of experiments from which other communities can benefit.

2. **Programs may be discrete, but problems require integrated responses.** Public social, educational, and economic programs are, by their nature, segmented by purpose and by administering agency. But people are not segmented, nor are the causes of social dysfunction. Consequently, the delivery of social services should be integrated at the local level, where the clients are, and be presented comprehensively.

3. **Formal contracts can be an effective way to ensure the commitment of all the parties at interest and can provide a democratic vehicle for solving problems.** Developed under quite general national guidance, the French innovation of the local contract is a valuable tool for assuring that all parties are clear about their objectives and the means for attaining them, that they have an opportunity to participate in crafting the program of local action, and that they have a template against which to evaluate the success of the program.

4. **The rehabilitation of housing has symbolic importance in disadvantaged communities, recreating a sense of "community."** As pride of place grows, pride of self is rekindled, and individuals are motivated to make the investments in themselves needed to attain a higher degree of economic and social independence. The task of organizing, financing, and undertaking neighborhood improvement projects has benefits far beyond the relatively simple act of "beautification."

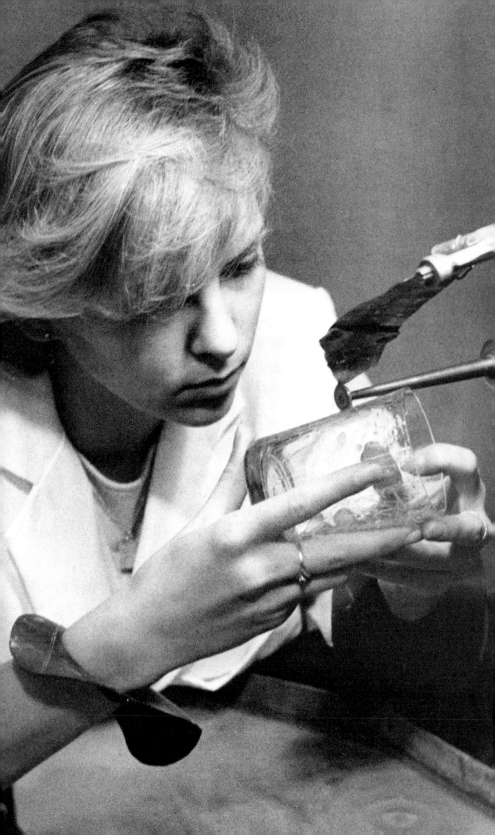

# CHAPTER 5

# GREAT BRITAIN:
## Rehabilitating the "Sick Man of Europe"

*Just downriver from Big Ben and Tower Bridge, the River Thames, running muddy and fast, bends first south, then north, forming a huge oxbow. Cupped within this curving reach of river is an area of East London, several miles across, long known as the Isle of Dogs—originally the "isle of docks:" a vast maze of wharves, warehouses, and channels, with the biggest area of enclosed docking water in Europe. From the Victorian era through World War II this area, known today simply as "the Docklands," was the heart of the British maritime empire. But after the war, with the coming of containerships too large to negotiate the river, the shipping industry declined and the Docklands followed.*

*Today, much of the area looks like a war zone. Towering loading cranes stand rusting above rotting docks. The shells of massive warehouses sit, windowless and often roofless, amid acres of rubble. Wide areas are simply empty, as if a bomb had leveled them. Here and there, an individual building—a perfectly preserved Georgian pub, or an ornate Victorian elementary school—stands alone in the middle of an empty block, with the isolated, distracted air of an old age pensioner who has lost his way.*

*Off on the western horizon, in the part of the Docklands closest to London's financial district, a glass-sheathed skyscraper glitters in the sun, surrounded by new, post-modernist apartment and office buildings and linked to central London by an elevated light rail system. Rising above the dusty wasteland, the new development looks like some city of the future.*

*Which is exactly what its developers hope it will be. This is the new Docklands—the largest redevelopment project in the world today. Only 5 miles from London's financial district, the Docklands is seen by its proponents in central government and in the development industry as the answer to London's chronic housing shortage and office congestion.*

*That this vision is not universally cherished is documented by the graffiti scrawled throughout the area: "Yuppies Out!" "Class Warfare!" and "Housing, Not Speculation!"*

*The project, and the controversy, began in 1981 when then-Secretary of State for Environment Michael Heseltine announced the creation of the London Docklands Development Corporation. Heseltine noted that the area represented "a major opportunity for development; for new housing, new environment, new industrial development, new facilities for recreation, new commercial development, new architecture." He also told Parliament that the Docklands "can only be successfully regenerated by a single-minded development agency"—by which he meant an organization that could overrule the objections of the Labour Party-dominated local planning authorities in East London's boroughs, receive tax incentives and financial support from central government, and seize property by eminent domain.*

*Having gotten off to a rocky start, things got rockier. Housing was indeed built, but predominantly for up-and-coming executives from the nearby financial district. Amenities were developed—sculpture, floating restaurants, windsurfing and artifical skiing facilities—but they held little attraction for East London's working-class families. Old businesses were squeezed out by Compulsory Purchase Orders or rising land prices and few new jobs went to locals. In fact, unemployment in the Docklands actually increased.*

*In the last three years, however, the controversy has begun to give way to collaboration. Local officials, developers, central government, schools, and community organizations have begun to work together on an array of new education, employment, and training reform programs aimed at ensuring that some of the 50,000 jobs still to be created by the project will go to East Londoners. Many of these programs have nationwide coverage, but the Docklands and East London's boroughs have become a highly-visible proving ground. There is still enough controversy to go around, but in many ways, the rehabilitation of London's Docklands—both the good and the bad—has been symbolic of the rehabilitation of the entire British economy.*

# The "Sick Man" Revives

In 1979, when Margaret Thatcher moved into 10 Downing Street, the "British Disease"—a sluggish economy characterized by low worker productivity, struggling nationalized industries, high unemployment, high inflation (reaching 24 percent in 1975), low levels of investment—was well advanced. The new Prime Minister was elected to bring about a change for the better, but as it turned out, things would get worse before they would get better. The Thatcher Government cut state subsidies to nationalized industries and, predictably, they began to collapse. Many social programs were slashed. Interest rates were hiked to quash consumer borrowing. In 1979, roughly 1 million people were unemployed; today, unemployment is somewhere between 3 and 4 million, depending upon whether people in a variety of government training and temporary employment schemes are counted.

It was bitter medicine indeed, but Britain's ailing economy did respond. During the last several years it has grown faster than that of any other European country—grown, in fact, at at rate roughly equal to Japan's. Inflation dropped from more than 13 percent in 1979 to under 5 percent (though it climbed back up to 8.3 percent by mid-1989). In a nation which traditionally looks down its nose at "new money," small business development is booming, with net new business formations rising from 16,000 a year in 1979 to 45,000 last year.

All this silver lining, however, is enveloped by a persistently dark cloud. The recent growth of new businesses is concentrated in the southern part of the country, near London, and it has not offset the massive job losses in Britain's largest industries and major industrial cities in the Midlands and the North. The unemployment rate is hovering around 8 percent nationwide and well over 10 percent in northern cities. In many minority neighborhoods, it is much higher. To be fair, Mrs. Thatcher's cutbacks did coincide with a "baby boom" peak in young people attempting to enter the workforce.

But at bottom, Britain's unemployment problem has less to do with the quantity of its workforce than with its quality, and an array of new initiatives aims at improving workforce competence.

# The Youth Training Scheme: Backing into the Future

*Initially, at least, we came from a starting point of
using training programs to keep unemployed
young people off the street. But we have shifted
our focus from unemployment to employment.*

—Geoffrey Holland
Permanent Secretary of State for Employment

To a great extent, Britain's economy has been a captive of its own early economic success. Having spawned the Industrial Revolution and grown rich from it, Britain was slow to respond when the revolution moved on in the latter half of the 20th century. Even as the contraction or collapse of major industries eliminated hundreds of thousands of low- and semi-skilled jobs, Britain's schools continued to mass-produce poorly skilled workers suited to the economy of a bygone industrial era.

Only 16 percent of compulsory school graduates in Britain go on to universities (compared to 57 percent in the United States). Fully two-thirds of all compulsory school graduates simply leave education at age 16, and a substantial number of them, according to Employment Secretary Holland, "have little to show for the time they spent in school." With substandard educations and no "dual system" by which to obtain labor market skills, many go directly from school to the dole.

In 1981, the government embarked upon a new training initiative seeking to: (1) create opportunities for employed and unemployed adults to update, expand, or strengthen their skills: (2) assure trainees certified standards of skill; and (3) encourage young people to pursue either further education or formal training until at least age 18.

Efforts on behalf of adults were only marginally successful, but the government's Youth Training Scheme (YTS), offering 16 and 17 year-olds up to two years of training and work experience, grew rapidly. The two-year YTS program provides an average of 25 weeks of off-the-job training, in addition to on-the-job training and planned work experience, leading towards recognized vocational qualifications. Trainees receive a modest, tax-free training allowance, but the principal benefit is direct contact with employers participating in the program. There are roughly 450,000 young people in YTS today.

YTS demonstrated, however, what many employers already knew: that compulsory school graduates were woefully unprepared to enter the world of work. It became clear that if Britain was to create a skilled, work-ready workforce, it would have to begin well before young people left school—creating better "products" in the first place, rather than repairing them after the fact.

## TVEI: Preparing Students For the World of Work

*When two-thirds of your trainees have never even handled a telephone, training must begin earlier and very basically.*

—Julia Cleverdon,
Director of Education, Business In The Community

The English educational system has had a long tradition of having little to do with the world of work. For centuries, the well-to-do have sent their children to school (exclusive private schools) to learn how to become gentlemen, not businesspeople. The working classes left school at the earliest opportunity. Even today, manufacturers complain about the continuing rigidity of the "classical" British education in the face of marketplace demands for technical competence.

In 1983, when it had become clear that post-graduation training programs like YTS could not hope to overcome the inadequacies of a compulsory school curriculum that provided little exposure to the world of work, the Thatcher government began a series of educational reforms. The first was a pilot Technical and Vocational Education Initiative (TVEI) introduced in a number of Local Education Authorities (LEAs) and aimed at increasing the problem-solving skills, initiative, enterprise, and creativity of 14 to 18 year-olds.

In language echoing the objectives of Sweden's education and training initiatives, TVEI's purpose was to create educational experiences that:

- Encourage students to stay in school and achieve nationally-recognized qualification levels which will be valuable to them—and which they see as valuable—when they make the transition to adult life;

- Use every opportunity to relate education to the world of work, using work experience, work shadowing, community projects and so on;
- Ensure that students' educational experiences are balanced and include exposure to the kind of technologies that, increasingly, will be part of their lives;
  - Improve their effectiveness as people by building self-confidence, independence, and adaptability to change;
- Develop positive attitudes towards industry, commerce, and community.

Participating LEAs are encouraged to pursue a high degree of experimentation. This could include sharing expert faculty, allowing students to move between schools to take advantage of special program offerings, creating regional centers of expertise, and establishing a wide array of linkages with industry. In some schools, industrialists act as curriculum advisors, tutors, or student advisors, and work experience is a critical component in all programs.

Newham Borough is one of the working-class neighborhoods in the shadow of the Docklands development district. In 1986, with unemployment stuck at 20 percent and the number of unemployed 16 to 19 year-olds nearly the highest in London, Newham—which had just attained the dubious honor of being the most disadvantaged local government authority in England—joined TVEI. Under Newham's program, roughly 250 students in four schools will take core courses (academic, personal, social, and health courses) and then be able to choose two of four more technical/vocational, courses of study. These include craft and design technology; art, design, and graphic communication; business studies and information technologies; and technology sciences.

Newham Borough's objectives are to create courses that are student-centered and relevant to the world around them; improve the school-to-work transition for students beyond compulsory school age (those 16 to 18); create a balanced curriculum which includes a wider range of subjects; build modern technical facilities for schools; and provide equal opportunities for girls (who have tended to be excluded from technical education in the past).

The rapid growth of the TVEI programs, and the government's commitment to them, is stunning. By 1987, nearly all LEAs in England, Wales, and Scotland had at least one TVEI program underway. By 1992, TVEI will be universal—that is, available in all secondary schools and for all students. By 1997, the government will have committed nearly one billion pounds to the TVEI program.

Whether TVEI will help Britain's young people find useful work and rewarding careers remains to be seen—and depends not just upon TVEI itself but upon whether the opportunities created by expansion of the nation's economy can be spread to the disadvantaged neighborhoods of London and the North. But clearly the efforts to involve industry, to reconstitute the curriculum to be more relevant to realities in the working world, and to build work experience into the regular compulsory school experience, have the potential of improving opportunities for young people, and strengthening disadvantaged neighborhoods in the bargain.

What's more, it has paved the way for other school-business community partnerships just now being implemented.

### *Partnerships and Compacts: Seeking Competitiveness, Businesses Discover Schools*

As recently as 10 years ago, connections between businesses and educational institutions in Britain were so infrequent as to be insignificant. Moreover, the deep-seated antipathy between government and organized labor resulted in the elimination of formal apprenticeship programs within unions.

Still, business and education were drawn together in the early 1980s when a few leading companies began to be concerned about long-term structural unemployment, inner-city unrest, and a pervasive anti-business attitude among British workers—especially young people. Several organizations were created through which businesses became involved in community and economic development issues. A number of businesses and business organizations, supported by an array of new government-sponsored enterprise schemes, turned to fostering small business development in disadvantaged areas as a way to inject new life into aging local economies.

But business executives soon discovered that the education and skill levels of the people they sought to help were so low that enterprise development was often not a realistic option. That discovery, combined with two other developments—a one-third drop in the number of 16 to 18 year olds by 1994, and the competitiveness challenge pose by the 1992 integration of EC markets—led the business community to direct participation in, and partnerships with, local education authorities.

The London Enterprise Agency (LENTA) illustrates this shift in policy direction. LENTA was one of the first of what today are more than 300 business-led enterprise organizations involved in business-education partnerships. Created in 1979 by 17 major corporations to foster new enterprise development within London's inner-city, LENTA had little to do with schools until a 1984 visit to David Rockefeller's New York Partnership convinced LENTA executives that businesses had an important stake in improving the education and skill levels of school-leavers. The coincidental release of a report by the Inner London Education Authority calling for closer working relationships between schools and the business community brought LENTA and ILEA together in a common purpose.

Then, in 1986, LENTA, ILEA, and London Docklands Development Corporation officials visited Boston and returned determined to establish a business-schools partnership similar to the Boston Compact. The three organizations first formed a London Education/Business Partnership and then, in September 1987, launched the London Compact. The first phase focuses on two boroughs bordering the Docklands. Like the Boston original, the London Compact involves a three-way commitment: students set goals and commit to pursuing them through school; schools commit to both students and business that they will provide opportunities to develop worklife-relevant skills; and companies commit to provide graduating students with a job and training or training with a job to follow. During the school year, the employers provide "work shadowing" opportunities for teachers and work experience for pupils, and they help develop the curriculum.

To date, 23 corporations and agencies have developed guarantees with 500 young people in four East London schools. In the participating schools, the dropout rate below age 16 has been cut from 25 percent to 15 percent. In addition, some 200 students have chosen to stay on in school for further education and training through age 18. Three more schools will join the London Compact this year.

Shortly after the London Compact was created, the Thatcher government embraced the concept and made compacts a national component of the Prime Minister's Inner City Initiative. By June 1988, proposals had been received from most inner-city areas in the nation and a month later 30 compacts were announced—twice the number originally planned—including five more in the London area. Early evidence suggests that compacts have been most successful in communities where some form of business-education partnership was already in place.

The latest stage in the evolution of business-education partnerships to emerge in Britain is a proposal to create local Training and Enterprise Councils (TECs), largely modelled on America's Private Industry Councils (PICs). Like their U.S. counterparts, the TECs will plan and control (but not actually run) local vocational training. Unlike the PICs, however, TECs would control the delivery of all government training programs for the unemployed and oversee courses offered by further education colleges. The TECs would be dominated by employers, with minority representation by local government and education authorities.

## Policy vs. Practice: Community Partnerships

In roughly ten years, Britain has redefined the relationships between education and the nation's economy. In the process, it has developed an aggressive human investment program, first moving away from income maintenance in favor of training the unemployed; then providing post-graduation training for school leavers to try to keep them from becoming unemployed; then reaching back into the school curriculum itself to increase the work-relevance of education in the final years of school to smooth the entry of young people to the labor market; and now creating compacts to reach students at an even earlier stage in their development and guarantee them work and further training when they do leave school.

The latest development is a sweeping reform of the structure of education in Britain. Education has long been decentralized in

Britain, in sharp contrast to the situation in France, for example. Most decisions are made by individual schools, with broad policy and staffing decisions controlled by local government through Local Education Authorities (LEA). Last year, however, the Thatcher government, in one of its most controversial actions to date, moved to change dramatically both the substance and the management of Britain's elementary and secondary schools.

The education bill included among many reforms: a comprehensive national core curriculum; the creation of uniform standards of performance and achievement for young people based on testing at ages 7, 11, 14, and 16; the development of standards of performance for teachers; the addition of parents to the governing bodies of schools, and of employers to the governing bodies of colleges and universities; and a provision permitting the governing bodies of schools to "go private"—detach themselves from local education authorities.

These reforms have sparked a high-decibel national debate, the heart of which is the charge that the Prime Minister is simply trying to weaken or eliminate local authorities, which tend to have Labour Party majorities.

As a practical matter, however, despite the polarization at the national level caused by these changes, at the local level, where the work has to get done, there is often remarkable collaboration between individuals and agencies with very different political ideologies. The London Education/Business Partnership is one example. LENTA officially characterizes the Inner London Education Authority as "very left-wing" and, no doubt, the ILEA would characterize LENTA as deeply conservative. Yet the economic and social challenge of East London posed practical problems that only practical partnerships could solve. And it is not simply a marriage of convenience; the continuing collaboration has brought a wide array of new initiatives to the Docklands and its surrounding boroughs.

The city of Leicester, in the East Midlands, is a good example. Leicester's economy is more diversified than many other Midlands or Northern industrial cities, but it still suffers significant mismatches between the skills of school-leavers and job requirements. In part for this reason, the unemployment level among young people age 16 to 19 is roughly 40 percent. Many of the unemployed are minorities who face language and social barriers as well.

At the political level, Leicester's city council, which has a large Labour Party majority, is categorically opposed to the policies of the Thatcher government. But at the operational level, Leicester has been adept at using each new education and training program developed by the central government as a new resource for achieving local objectives: improving wealth creation and wealth distribution. Leicester, for example, has a comprehensive array of YTS programs. All Leicester schools are involved in TVEI. In part because of their tradition of local collaboration, Leicester was well-prepared to be one of the first cities to implement a business/education compact. In fact, Leicester's long-standing Education/Industry Committee had developed a 5-year plan envisioning compacts (among many other initiatives) before the national government had begun considering them as a vehicle for improving secondary education and the school-to-work transition.

Another reason Leicester has been able to move so quickly to rehabilitate both its education and its training programs—both for young people and adults—is the city's long tradition of "community schools." Ironically, the success of Britain's newest education reforms may well depend on the foundation laid by one of its oldest education reforms—the community school.

### The British Community School: A New Heart for an Aging Economy

*To think of it as a "school" is to fail to grasp how integrated with the community it is. . .*

—Tommy Masters of the Cranford Community School

*The community school seeks to obliterate the boundary between the community and the school, to turn the community into a school and the school into a community.*

—A. H. Halsey of Oxford University

In the heart of Hounslow Borough, on London's western edge and a mile or so from from the flight path of Heathrow Airport, sits the Cranford Community School—a small "campus" of one- and two-story brick buildings surrounded by playing fields. The pupils, age 11 through 18 and dressed in neat blue uniforms, are predominantly Sikh immigrants. But at certain times of the day, they are outnumbered by adults from surrounding neighborhoods for whom this "high school" is also a recreation center, training center, meeting place, job placement center, and health service— even a "pub" in the evening. Cranford was Greater London's first comprehensive "community school," and it remains a leader today in educational innovation.

The notion that a school might serve as something more than just a place where children are educated has a long tradition in Britain, emerging first in Cambridgeshire in the 1920s and spreading to nearby Leicestershire, Nottinghamshire, and Coventry, and then nationwide. While "community schools" or "community colleges," as they have been known, have been sources of continuing education for adults, their core role has generally been more social than economic. In the last two decades, however, the sluggishness of the British economy, high levels of unemployment, and rapid change in the kinds of skills needed for workers to be competitive in the labor market, have created new roles for community schools and colleges throughout Britain. Today they are places where a wide range of public services, from training and literacy development to health and recreation, can be offered to meet community needs and improve opportunity for all residents. Increasingly, they are the heart of the neighborhoods in which they are located, and a proving ground for the newest education and training reforms.

Community schools, like all secondary schools in Britain, serve young people age 11 to 16, for whom school is compulsory, as well as so-called "Sixth Form," or sixth year, students (age 16–18). Until recently, the Sixth Form was primarily for academic or technical students going on to higher education, but today, as many as 50 percent of the young people who might have left school at 16 in the past are staying on to improve their skills, take additional subjects that meet their needs, or earn a higher-grade diploma.

At community schools, however, these school-age young people are joined by other young people participating in YTS and other training initiatives, as well as adults who use the school to meet a wide array of needs. Roughly half of all the LEAs in Britain have at least one community school/ college and half of those have several. The industrial city of Coventry, for example, has nine.

At Cranford, the winner of several national education and training awards, programs offered include at least the following, though programs change as community needs evolve:

- **Adult Education:** some 800-1,000 adults make use of 12-week courses offered evenings and weekends;

- **Open University:** the school is one of many "Open University" centers in the nation, serving the needs of some 150 enrolled adults one day per week;

- **Women's Training Program:** over 100 women interested in returning to the job market after raising a family take 12-week courses. Courses are offered in the morning and a nursery is provided for students' children. Some 70 percent of the women attending these courses have obtained jobs;

- **Sixth Form Courses for Adults:** a specific program designed to permit adults to obtain secondary-school certificates;

- **Job Training:** the school conducts courses for British Airways to upgrade the basic skills of would-be employees (who receive some money from the government while they are being trained—which may be augmentedby the company); provides off-the-job training courses for future employees of Heathrow's Freight Forwarding companies (candidates are recruited by the companies, paid to attend the course, then hired); offers English language proficiency courses for hotel and restaurant companies with non-English speaking employees; and operates other training programs either run jointly with government and private industry, or custom-crafted for local companies;

- **The Print Shop:** the school produces a weekly newspaper for the community, in the process training a number of long-term unemployed individuals who subsequently find work in the printing field;

- **Nursery/Daycare:** the school operates a self-supporting nursery/daycare program for women taking courses at the school;

- **"Mums and Toddlers" Program:** this community outreach program is designed to provide opportunities for young, often socially isolated mothers to get to know other mothers in the community and pursue common interests;

- **Community Recreation Center:** the sports facilities at the school serve 112 recreational groups and some 3,000 to 4,000 adults (on a fee basis) each week;
- **Youth Program:** the school serves as the community meeting center for a wide variety of clubs and other social organizations for young people, age 11–21;
- **Gypsies Community Center Program:** one evening a week, the school operates a social and community outreach program for "gypsies"—itinerant families who set up camps in nearby fields;
- **Health Clinic:** the school operates a neighborhood health clinic, staffed by two full-time nurses provided by the local health authority and one provided by the school and a part-time doctor who visits on a regular schedule;
- **Space Leasing:** the school leases out its space for private and community functions.

In all, some 6,000 adults use the facilities of the Cranford Community School in any given week—as many as 400 during the day, and the balance evenings and weekends. In contrast, secondary school pupils in the school number about 1,000.

Like most community schools, Cranford has three deputy heads: one for academics, a second for student affairs, and a third for community programs. Funding for many of these programs is highly entrepreneurial and many programs are designed to bring in new money to underwrite broadened services. Most of the training programs are funded by government or quasi-governmental organizations like the Training Agency (formerly the Manpower Services Commission), either directly or indirectly. Sometimes government training funds are funnelled to the school through private companies. A few others are funded directly by private industry.

The result of the integration of school needs and community needs is that community schools are especially adept both at ensuring that education is relevant to the world graduates will enter, and at providing a wide array of adult education, training, and job search services to help individuals already out of school to develop the skills they need in order to compete in a fast-changing economy. In this regard, Cranford is not unique; community schools throughout the nation serve similar purposes, the details varying with the needs of the community served by each.

Cranford, for example, sits in an area of England that has a booming economy. Consequently, the mix of programs it offers differs from those offered, for example, by the Erresford Grange Community School, which serves a neighborhood in Coventry still reeling from the effects of industrial restructuring. At Erresford Grange, greater emphasis is placed on providing daytime recreational opportunities for out-of-work adults and, once they are there, on retraining programs available through the school.

## A Question of Direction

Britain's commitment to a radical restructuring of its education and training systems, and its willingness to move expeditiously and to make significant long-term investments to achieve its objectives, are impressive.

And yet there is much that is puzzling about Britain's approach. In a number of ways, the process by which Britain is attempting to reach its objectives is the direct antithesis of those taken by several other European nations. First, while a remarkable degree of bipartisan agreement exists in much of Europe over both the objectives and the procedures for improving the work-readiness of young people, Britain's programs are characterized by an equally remarkable level of antagonism between the government and several of the other key players in education and training reform. Britain, like the other nations, speaks often of "partnerships," but in fact, in Britain only two partners count: government and industry. Local governments and labor organizations not only are not invited to the table, but significant effort is exerted by government to eliminate them from the issue entirely. Where they do exist, true local partnerships appear to exist in spite of central government policy, not as a result of it.

Second, and closely related, the changes that have been made in the last decade have been almost exclusively "top-down"—delivered by central government with little local involvement. Even as other European nations strive to decentralize decisionmaking and increase the role of communities and local authorities in the formulation of policy on education and training, Britain has increasingly centralized these activities. The Thatcher government would no doubt argue that the situation is dire and that aggressive action is needed—all of which is true. But the absence of efforts to create localized solutions would appear to invite programs that are unnecessarily rigid and insensitive to local variations in conditions and likely solutions.

Third, the pace of new education and training policy development in Britain is so rapid that there appears to be little opportunity for evaluating either the effectiveness of existing programs or the wisdom of new ones—many of which appear to be borrowed unchanged from the United States. Again, the urgency to act is clear. Yet the urgency is as great in other European nations. The strength of the Swedish and West German approaches to these same challenges has been their willingness to test, revise, retest, and only then implement new initiatives nationwide. The result is a minimum of unforeseen consequences, the opportunity to build consensus, and thus a degree of stability in the midst of change. In contrast, Britain's virtual "overnight" adoption of both the compact and the private industry council appears to have given little attention to the acknowledged problems that have been encountered with both programs in the United States. The effect of these rapid shifts in policy and programs is an atmosphere of "churning," rather than thoughtful change.

## Lessons from Britain

Despite these reservations, several of Britain's education and training innovations present important lessons for improving the quality of education and training:

1. **The school-business connection is crucial to improving the relevance of education and assuring young people a place in the working world when they complete their schooling.** It is a two-way street: the school-business linkage strengthens the quality and relevance of the educational experience and produces graduates more capable of meeting the skill needs of an increasingly competitive economy.

2. **Ideological conflict need not create operational conflict.** The ideological differences between Britain's Conservative-

dominated central government and Labour-dominated local governments could not be more sharply defined. And yet in some communities (like Leicester) the commonality of local concerns has bridged the ideological chasm. Local partnerships composed of central government agency representatives, local agencies, school officials, parents, businesspeople, labor unions, and others have succeeded in creating operational reforms that achieve the often very different aims of the partners, while benefitting the community as a whole.

3. **A school can play many roles.** A secondary school can be a multiple use environment: a community services delivery center, a networking center for solving community problems, and an enabler and empowerer of individuals of all ages—through education, training, literacy, health, self-esteem building and other programs. The more roles the school plays, the more it serves as the heart of the community and the better it serves the needs of its "students"—children, young people, adults, and seniors.

4. **"Going to school" is a more attractive experience for young people and adults alike when the school itself is a multiple use facility.** The more closely it is linked to other community activities, to business, to people of all ages, the more enriched and relevant the experience of attending, and the better the school in the long run.

5. **The community school is especially valuable in areas experiencing rapid economic change.** The more wrenching the shifts in the local economy, the more important a comprehensive, integrated, business- and community-linked school is to helping individuals and neighborhoods adapt to and benefit from change.

# CHAPTER 6

# WEPIC:
# Neighbors Reinvent the Public School

*A walk down 60th Street in West Philadelphia is a profoundly unsettling experience. Clearly it was once a thriving neighborhood—before the flight to the suburbs emptied so many of the two-story row houses on the side-streets, shuttered so many of the stores, closed so many of the small businesses that gave the area its sense of community. What remains today is the pervasive seediness common to all disadvantaged neighborhoods: the peeling paint, the sagging aluminum awnings, the windows covered with plywood, doors clad in iron grillwork or blocked entirely with sheetmetal or cinderblock, the debris of poverty underfoot— fast food wrappers, beer cans, pint bottles of liquor. Easily two-thirds of 60th Street's storefronts are boarded up and the businesses that remain are incongruous: several real estate offices and a remarkable number of churches—storefront Baptist churches, an Episcopal church, the Church of the Open Door, the Kingdom Hall of the Jehovah's Witnesses, and more—places of hope on a street that seems to have little to hope for.*

*But despite the obvious decline, despair is not the predominant mood on 60th Street. Instead, there is a pervasive sense that the entire neighborhood is holding its breath. Waiting for something. Watching for a sign.*

*What people in West Philly are watching for is a shift in the fortunes of the neighborhood. A turnaround. And if you turn off 60th onto some of the sidestreets, the signs of change are there—small ones, to be sure, but signs nevertheless. Turn onto Hazel Avenue, and along the sidewalks there are wooden planters with evergreen shrubs and, occasionally, bright petunias. Turn onto Cedar, and there is attractive landscaping around the William Cullen Bryant Elementary School—and a mural encircling walls once covered with graffiti. Turn onto Osage and, near the corner and across the street from what only a few months ago was a thriving "crack house," a team of black high school kids is putting the final touches on an abandoned row house they have spent the last year rebuilding, under the guidance of retired white union carpenter Walt McAuley. A few blocks away at "West," as West Philadelphia High School is known, other kids are building a greenhouse, landscaping and painting the school, rebuilding an historic pipe organ, and starting their own in-school store. At H.C. Lea Middle School, similar projects are underway.*

*Vandalism, random violence, and drugs are still a way of life on 60th Street. Unemployment and welfare dependency are still high, as are teen pregnancy and infant mortality. But in West Philadelphia's schools, and in the neighborhoods around them, small projects, designed by students, teachers, parents, and other individuals and organizations that make up the West Philly community, are creating meaningful jobs for young people—jobs that connect their schoolwork to the real world and that redefine the role of public schools in the revitalization of disadvantaged neighborhoods.*

## *Out of the Ashes: WEPIC's Birth by Fire*

On May 13, 1985, responding to escalating complaints by residents in the Osage Avenue area of West Philadelphia, public authorities took steps to evict the members of a shadowy radical group called MOVE from their derelict, garbage-strewn row house. The group resisted and, in an abortive attempt to force them out, an explosive device was dropped on the roof. The building caught fire, the fire spread rapidly, and soon a several block area was engulfed. Homes burned, people died, children were traumatized, families were displaced—the fabric of the community, already threadbare, was reduced to ashes.

As is often the case, the tragedy of the MOVE fire focused new attention on the social and economic condition of the West Philadelphia neighborhood where the fire occurred—an area of classic urban distress: high unemployment, low median family income, heavy dependency on Aid to Families with Dependent Children and other public assistance programs, high rates of teenage pregnancy and exceptionally high levels of infant mortality, poor housing, low education levels, and—not surprisingly—high levels of drug use and crime. According to the 1980 Census, the census tracts in the community included two "close to distress," five "below distress," and 10 "below the poverty level."

The prospects for children growing up in the neighborhood—never very bright—were dimming. Dropout rates were high and even those who completed school faced bleak employment prospects because their literacy skills and work habits were poorly developed. West Philadelphia's children were becoming part of what the nationally-acclaimed report *Children in Need: Investment Strategies for the Educationally Disadvantaged* called "a permanent underclass."

Long before the MOVE fire, four University of Pennsylvania students in an undergraduate history honors seminar led by President Sheldon Hackney, noted historian Lee Benson, and Ira Harkavy, Vice Dean of the School of Arts and Sciences and Director of the Office of Community-Oriented Policy Studies, proposed developing an education and youth employment program that would use neighborhood revitalization projects as a way of motivating young people to stay in school and provide them basic job-related skills while involving and improving the community in which they lived. By creating a school- and community-based "learning-by-doing" improvement program, the Penn students hoped to build both individual self-esteem and community pride while strengthening the practical skills of the participants. They reasoned that students' future prospects were directly related to their willingness to stay in school; that their willingness to stay in school was based on their perception of the relevance of what they were learning to the world in which they lived; and that much of what they were learning in conventional elementary and high school education did not meet that test.

The Penn students proposed creating a West Philadelphia Improvement Corps—initially 50 young people in five West Philadelphia neighborhoods working on small community improvement projects under the supervision of teachers working after school and during the summer. The project, known as "WEPIC," would be a part of the West Philadelphia Partnership, an existing coalition of institutions of higher education, corporations, and community service organizations dedicated to improving conditions in West Philadelphia.

In the wake of the MOVE confrontation and fire, the program was expanded to include an additional 62 young people from the affected area and the project focused its attention on the neighborhood where the fire had occurred.

Symbolically, WEPIC chose as its emblem the phoenix, rising from the ashes, borne on the hands of many people working together.

## From University Theory to Community Reality: WEPIC Grows

By June 1985, WEPIC had changed from a University seminar concept to a reality, organized under the umbrella of the West Philadelphia Partnership and funded by small grants from The Philadelphia Office of Employment Training and the UPS Foundation.

Teachers and community supervisors spent several weeks overseeing groups of local middle school and high school students in the area most affected by the fire. Focusing their work around the neighborhood Bryant Elementary School, with the assistance of adults from neighboring houses, they planted trees around the school, did cleanup and landscaping, and replaced graffiti on the school's exterior walls with murals.

At the same time, University students in Penn's Public Service Summer Internship Program worked as administrators for the program and began designing what would become an after-school program in the fall. By fall 1985, the two Bryant School teachers involved in the project were already "teaching WEPIC"—that is, using WEPIC projects (including community history surveys of residents, periodic Bryant Clean-Up Days, the creation of Christmas wreaths for the families displaced by the MOVE fire, and maintenance of the new plantings) to teach students math, science, and social studies. Freed from abstract classroom instruction and able to connect the concepts they were learning with the projects they were doing, students' learning levels increased.

By spring 1986, two more schools—West Philadelphia High School and H.C. Lea Elementary School had joined WEPIC and the program had received additional funding support from The Samuel S. Fels Foundation and Hunt Manufacturing, a Philadelphia-based firm. During the previous academic year, Penn's Annenberg School of Communications produced a film on the project and landscape assistance was offered by the Department of Landscape Architecture. By summer, projects were underway in all three schools. At Bryant, a neighborhood council composed of residents, church officials, and business leaders began developing a major landscaping project for the school, working with a landscape architecture student at the University. At West, other teams were working on painting, flower and vegetable gardens, creating half-barrel planters with evergreen trees for school entrances, and recycling projects. At Lea, graffiti was removed and murals were painted on exterior school walls. In all, there were six teachers from three schools, and 35 students employed in the neighborhood and school improvement projects.

With the additional support of the Philadelphia Private Industry Council, WEPIC moved into the fall 1986 term with a significant after-school program. Three teachers and 30 students at West worked during the school year on maintaining the new gardens around the school, doing interior and exterior painting, developing hydroponic gardening, designing and painting a mural at the Philadelphia Zoo, and participating in pre-employment training programs, resume-writing, job application-writing, and interviewing workshops. One teacher and 11 students at Lea worked on similar programs. At Bryant, planning for the major landscaping project continued.

Attracting increasing local and national attention, by spring 1987 WEPIC had received additional funding from the Fels Foundation and the Sun Company Foundation, and had been chosen by the U.S. Department of Labor as a National Demonstration Youth Employment and Training Program. The Labor Department grant was for WEPIC's most ambitious project yet: 20 students at West, working closely with an industrial arts teacher, a social studies teacher, and union craftspeople, would rehabilitate, landscape, and sell a property at 6009 Osage Avenue, just a block from the site of the MOVE fire. Once again, the University played a major role: the design of the demonstration project was originally developed by students at the 1986 Public Service Summer Internship Program.

In the spring and summer of 1987, as the rehab project got underway, the schools were busy with other projects as well. Bryant's landscaping project was completed; the restoration of West's massive and historic pipe organ began (with the assistance of a specialist); a team of WEPIC students worked on a summer-long project at the Philadelphia Zoo; and a variety of maintenance, gardening, painting, and poster/mural projects were completed. In all, more than 100 students were employed in WEPIC projects.

With additional support from the Charles Stewart Mott Foundation and the United Way, by fall 1987 the concept of "teaching WEPIC"—of embedding academic skill development within the projects sponsored by WEPIC and using the projects as classroom teaching devices—was well-established at all three schools. Also during this period, other schools began to express interest in joining WEPIC activities; the first to do so was the John P. Turner Middle School.

By the spring of 1988, additional funding from the Pennsylvania Department of Education permitted West to begin developing a "School Within A School" completely dedicated to the concept of using WEPIC projects as the vehicle for classroom education. As a beginning, West is using the creation of a greenhouse as the centerpiece for math and science instruction and construction skills development. While students in this program will continue to take four periods per day in math, science, social studies, and English/literacy lab, the balance of the day will be devoted to the application of these skills to the design and construction of the greenhouse. In addition, the U.S. Department of Labor renewed its National Demonstration Project commitment for the rehabilitation of the Osage Avenue property, and the carpenters union agreed to link WEPIC to its apprenticeship training program. Moreover, work continued on the pipe organ rehabilitation, and on other projects at Lea and Bryant School, along with painting and other improvement projects at Turner.

Additional support from the Mott Foundation and the State Department of Labor and Industry have permitted the expansion of several programs and, in the 1988 school year, the creation of a school store within West Philadelphia High School as yet another WEPIC employment/education initiative. By the beginning of the 1988 fall term, both the Andrew Hamilton and Add B. Anderson Elementary Schools joined the WEPIC program. In addition, The Center for Literacy asked the students and staff of West Philadelphia High School's "School-Within-A-School" program to build a literacy center in the basement of a neighborhood building.

Support from the German Marshall Fund of the United States permitted teachers, WEPIC staff, and city and state policymakers to meet with high-level government and education leaders in Sweden, West Germany, France, and Great Britain to discuss innovations in school-based training and community revitalization programs.

This experience, combined with research conducted by University of Pennsylvania undergraduates, led to a $600,000 grant from the State Department of Labor and Industry to the Philadelphia Private Industry Council in January 1989 to fund WEPIC to create "community schools" at both West Philadelphia High School and the John P. Turner Middle School. Designed not simply to educate students, the proposed "community schools" propose to operate 18 hours a day, 7 days a week, 12 months a year, as social, education and training centers for the community, providing job training programs, public health services, daycare programs, child care training and other programs for young mothers, and serving as a recreation center for the community, among other services.

### Small Steps Transform Students, Teachers, and a Community

*"The students working with WEPIC have acquired a sense of value and self-esteem that is unbelievable. They have taken pride in themselves, the school, and the community...They showed us daily that the lessons learned in the classroom were applicable to what they were doing with WEPIC. They made the connection! This is what education is all about—not only acquiring knowledge, but being able to apply that knowledge to everyday life."*

—Beth Showell, teacher, West Philadelphia High School

*WEPIC is especially important for a significant number of our students who rarely have the opportunity to experience success.*

—John W. Grellis, Principal, Henry C. Lea Elementary School

WEPIC does not choose participating students randomly. Nor does it "cream" the best students to ensure high success levels, the way many federally sponsored job training programs tend to do. For the most part, WEPIC students have below-average attendance records, poor academic achievement, and low self-esteem. Most come from families on welfare. Still, the results are startling: of the 28 West Philadelphia High School students involved in the project from May 1986 to June 1987, only one student dropped out of school (entering a Job Corps program in West Virginia)—a 3.5 percent dropout rate for WEPIC, compared to an approximately 17 percent dropout rate for the school as a whole. Moreover, there was a 100 percent promotion or graduation rate for the remaining WEPIC students.

But many of the changes underway in West Philadelphia's schools and neighborhoods are more difficult to quantify. WEPIC teachers in elementary and middle school report significant changes in the attitudes of their students. One WEPIC teacher reports: "Our students made remarkable social and emotional growth. They know they must set high goals for themselves, develop pride and self-confidence, build stronger life survival skills, and practice positive problem-solving techniques."

The teachers too are remotivated by participating in WEPIC, discovering again why it was they chose to become teachers in the first place. Says one teacher: "WEPIC has given me a new lease on my professional career. I would never have thought, 28 years ago when I began teaching, that at this point in my career I would be as eager to go forward as I am now."

WEPIC also has begun to change how residents in West Philadelphia feel about their neighborhood and their future. Small projects—graffiti removal, landscaping, a vegetable garden—have brought neighbors out of their homes to help, to provide tools, to protect improvements from vandals, to donate materials, and to organize themselves for additional, long-term neighborhood improvement projects independent of WEPIC.

## *The School as Neighborhood Focal Point*

*WEPIC focuses on two themes: the use of vocational education as a means of teaching basic academic subjects while also teaching vocational skills; and an emphasis on school and community improvement as a focus for curriculum content.*

—Dr. Marion B. W. Holmes, Executive Director, Division of Career and Vocational Education, Philadelphia

The core concept behind WEPIC is simply that a neighborhood school occupies a unique place in the community—it is neutral ground and everyone feels they own a part of it. Its job is not simply to educate children, but to build them, to empower them, to stoke their dreams and hone their skills. WEPIC teachers and administrators feel schools have the same responsibility to the community of which they are a part—to build and strengthen a community's identity, to be the center of the rehabilitation of community life. But over the years, schools have become so specialized, and so bureaucratized, that their connection to the community has weakened and the connections between education, work, and community life have been lost. Increasingly, they are seen by the young people they seek to serve as irrelevant. And children in disadvantaged communities are the first to spot the irrelevance. They look at the stark realities in the world around them, then at their schooling experience, find it mismatched, and drop out—foreclosing their options as adults, parents, and citizens in the process.

WEPIC uses local community development and improvement projects as a cure for irrelevance—as a tool for restoring community pride, building individual self-esteem, and helping students make the connection between schooling and achieving their dreams.

After only three years, WEPIC is still in its infancy. But it is proving a precocious child: having received first local, then national, and finally international recognition, WEPIC now seeks to make schools the life centers of their communities, offering not simply education for the neighborhood's children, but also daycare and health care centers, literacy programs, adult job training, and social and recreational programs.

In this regard WEPIC has evolved a role for public schools that echoes the education, youth employment, and community development initiatives underway in Sweden, West Germany, France, and Great Britain—increasing the skill levels of new entrants to the workforce and those already working, helping create avenues out of poverty for those who are unemployed or underemployed, and fostering community-wide physical, economic, and social revitalization.

# CHAPTER 7

# CONCLUSION
## Guiding Principles for Strengthening Workforce Competence in America

### *Competition and Cooperation*

It is difficult to overstate how seriously the European Community takes the challenge of creating a skilled and competitive workforce—particularly its commitment to youth employment and skill development. Since 1983, at least three formal EC-wide Action Programmes have been initiated, including:

- a program on the transition of young people from education to working life which focused on increasing school-industry partnerships;

- a program to raise the standards of post-compulsory school vocational training and ensure that it leads to recognized qualifications for young people with different ability levels; and

- a parallel program to upgrade the quality and work-relevance of compulsory education systems.

These initiatives, with multi-year budgets in the millions of dollars, are in addition to the efforts made by individual European nations, some of which have been described in these pages, to prepare young people for the world of work. What's more, they illustrate an important characteristic of the approach European nations have taken to the challenge of workforce competence: that while they continue to compete vigorously with each other, they are also working cooperatively to lift skill levels throughout the EC. This commitment to cooperation even extends to the provision of special technical assistance funds to less-developed members (Greece, Portugal, Spain, and Ireland) by the more advanced member nations.

Thus, to a greater or lesser degree throughout Western Europe, concerted effort to meet the youth employment and skill challenge is being pursued through *community-specific programs* aimed at populations or individuals with special education or skill problems; through *universal nationwide programs* designed to upgrade the quality of each country's workforce as a whole, with special emphasis on young people; and through *Europe-wide programs* aimed squarely at the workforce competitiveness issue at the heart of the planned 1992 integration of the Common Market.

It is not uncommon for U.S. policymakers to dismiss the innovative skill-building programs developed by some Western European nations as somehow unique to their respective cultures or more feasible because of their small size or (in several cases) the relative homogeneity of their populations. But the single-mindedness with which the EC as a whole is attacking the issue is impossible to ignore. There could hardly be more disparate voices or cultures than, for example, those of Great Britain and Greece, or West Germany and Portugal. Yet despite their differences they are united on the urgency of revolutionizing education and training programs today to increase the quality and competitiveness of tomorrow's workforce.

### Toward a Unified and Unifying American Vision

That school and job training officials from West Philadelphia found themselves studying youth employment and training programs in Europe illustrates a telling reality about youth education, training, and employment programs in the United States: while imaginative local initiatives exist in a number of forward-thinking communities (some of which, in fact, have been copied in Europe), coherent statewide approaches to the issue are relatively rare, and a unified national policy—a policy comparable to those in place in many European nations and in the EC as a whole—is conspicuously absent.

In its place, America has a largely directionless, and often rancorous debate. Industry leaders charge that public schools are a failure and that their graduates are unemployable. School officials argue that they cannot keep up with the shifting needs of employers and the diminishing role of parents. Elected officials proclaim the primacy of education, then plead budget constraints. Labor leaders are wary. Teachers feel besieged. Social services professionals warn of an increasingly permanent "underclass." The debate ranges across the individual component parts of the issue—illiteracy, dropout rates, teacher salaries, labor shortages, poverty and homelessness, crime and drug abuse, community deterioration, and so on—but fails to coalesce as a coherent policy on workforce competence.

And yet, the basic principles of a coherent, comprehensive policy exist. They exist within the national experiences of our European competitors and the local experiences of some of our own pioneering communities—communities like West Philadelphia. But the decibel level of the debates on component parts of the issue has tended to drown out these unifying principles.

As a practical matter, the task of increasing workforce competence cannot be "micro-managed" at the national level. Nationally managed programs demand homogeneous approaches in a world characterized by widely differing local conditions. They attempt to exert control by means of a predetermined set of often hypothetical conditions, and tend to be inflexible, employing nationally coordinated field audit teams to assure that local programs are not straying too far from "approved" approaches. The truth is, state and local officials, working with educators, employers, and labor leaders have the skills and sensitivity to develop the program most likely to work given local circumstances.

What these state and local entities need is a unified and unifying vision—a national declaration of purpose—based upon proven principles and backed by sufficient resources to turn that vision into successful, locally appropriate realities.

From the experiences profiled in the preceding pages, we can outline the basic principles that should inform that vision and guide local and state action.

### Guiding Principles for a
### Coherent National Policy on
### Workforce Education and Skill Development

*Principle #1: Work is a central defining element of human existence; cash income payments do not substitute for work.*

In Sweden, it is an article of faith. In West Germany it is a point of honor. In Britain, it is a lesson still being learned through painful and costly experience. The lesson is this: work builds self-respect and contributes to the economy; passive measures—income support without education and training—strips self-respect and impoverishes the economy.

Even in prosperous, rapidly-growing economies, some people will be left behind or left out. Leading European countries have concluded (often after having witnessed the failure of welfare programs far more generous than our own) that training and work strategies, not income maintenance programs, are the only effective way to bring these individuals back into the mainstream. Consequently, substantial public resources are spent to ensure—and in Sweden to guarantee—that young people leaving school are capable of obtaining work and that adults have the opportunity to acquire new skills when their old jobs are eliminated by economic change. In contrast to the United States, income maintenance programs tend to be a policy of last resort.

These programs require a significant political and financial commitment on the part of central government. But experience has shown that the cost of programs that reaffirm individual self-worth and build competence through further education, training, and work, is far outweighed by savings created from the prevention of costly social pathologies—crime, drug use, and other forms of individual or social violence.

***Principle #2:*** *Economic competitiveness depends upon creating and maintaining a world class universal educational system.*

Part of Europe's commitment to education and training investments—especially in smoothing the school-to-work transition—is simply cultural tradition. Sweden's work experience program for school students is decades old. Germany's "dual system" of private apprenticeships and public vocational training is centuries old. What is instructive about these systems, however, is not their longevity, but their adaptability. Where one might expect to find arthritic inflexibility, the reality is that these systems are responding well to change—particularly to Europe's deepening skilled labor shortage. Their leaders recognize that if their economies are to grow, no individual can afford to be left behind or precluded by inadequate education or skills from entering the labor force.

Recognizing that remediation is more difficult than initial education, many European nations, and the EC as a whole, are concentrating on wholesale reform of primary, secondary, and vocational educational systems to assure a seamless school-to-work transition—one which produces literate and technically skilled workers and guarantees rewarding work for every one of them, to the extent possible within the political context of each nation. Increasingly, the same commitment is being extended to individuals already in the workforce.

***Principle #3***: *Work experience and work-relevant education are the keys to smooth school-to-work transitions.*

Work experience related to the curriculum, and school courses relevant to the world of work, are the keys to the success of European efforts to smoooth the school-to-work transition. Not coincidently, these are also among the keys to the success of the West Philadelphia program, and many other effective local programs.

The specific methods vary from country to country and the EC is encouraging transnational cooperative partnerships. Sweden phases in work experience beginning at the primary school level and peaking in post-compulsory upper-secondary school, when young people may spend as much as 60 percent of their time in workplaces. In West Germany, a work experience component is built into the curriculum of compulsory secondary school and carried beyond compulsory school through the dual system. In Great Britain, work-relevant education now begins in compulsory school and is aided by the participation of the business community in curriculum development and compact-based post-graduation job and training guarantees. The variations aside, these nations, and others in the EC, are united in their recognition of the importance of ensuring that there are direct links between the world of school and the world of work.

***Principle #4***: *One outcome of education and training should be universally recognized and accepted skill credentials.*

The elimination of trade barriers between EC nations at the end of 1992 has made immediate and real a hitherto theoretical notion: that the workforce of the future should have "portable" skills. "1992" will create not just open markets for products and services, but for workers as well. Workers who want to ensure their employability, and governments that want to protect against unemployment and increase economic growth, both have a stake in the creation of training programs that lead to recognized standards of professionalism and quality. In Europe, the immediacy of 1992 has brought the key equation sharply into focus: quality guarantees competitiveness; workforce education and skill credentials guarantee quality. In the United States, no longer able to survive on its own domestic markets alone, the same equation applies.

**Principle #5:** *Creating the workforce of the future requires partnerships and private sector participation.*

Creating a highly skilled workforce requires partnerships at both the policymaking and operation levels. No one player—not government, not industry, not unions, not the local school system—can do it alone. Part of the reason is financial; the investments are huge. But the deeper reason is just as pragmatic: No one knows the answers; the right formula emerges from group collaboration.

This collaboration occurs on two levels. Policy emerges most successfully at the national level when developed cooperatively by the major stakeholders. Most of the nations examined here have well-established *policy partnerships* that, for example, develop broad national policies to strengthen education and training and increase working life experiences in the school curriculum. They cooperate because they recognize they have a common interest in the outcome. Indeed, the key parties—business, labor, and government—are often referred to as "the social partners." Britain appears to be the only exception among the countries examined: while partnerships are frequently invoked in national policy discussions about workforce skill development, in practice, some "partners" are clearly more equal than others. Government officials and business leaders develop policies; labor unions and local authorities are typically excluded.

At the local level, however, true *operational partnerships* emerge even in many British communities. All the stakeholders at the local level recognize that national administrations come and go, but problems persist and are felt most acutely at the community level. The challenge is to use the programmatic and financial building blocks provided by whomever is in power at the time to craft workable long-term solutions. In such situations, ideology typically gives way to pragmatics.

In the process of creating partnerships, one of the clearest lessons of the European training reforms—and one emerging from the experience of Private Industry Councils in the U.S.—is that business must play a significant role—both in financing training (as the principal direct beneficiary) and in influencing the content of educational curricula and training courses. Where training systems work best, in West Germany and Sweden for example, companies and trade unions have, after decades of tug and pull, come to view their training expenditures as strategic investments in long-term competitiveness, not as business costs.

Not surprisingly, policy and operational partnerships are also at the heart of the WEPIC program, and have been from the outset. WEPIC organizers sought an inclusive process for both designing and implementing the initiatives they have undertaken. Within the community, students, teachers, parents, and neighborhood businesses and organizations all play a part. Outside of the neighborhood itself, special attention has been given to ensure the involvement of key city and state agencies, teachers', building trades, and other labor unions, businesses and the Private Industry Council, foundations and city-wide organizations. The reasons are not principally financial; instead, WEPIC has sought to ensure that all the key players have a role in shaping the initiatives, a stake in the success of the program, and a chance to share in its successes.

***Principle #6:*** *Excellence cannot be parachuted into schools; it must be built from within.*

While national policy guidance is crucial, local development and control of specific operational programs is the only way to assure workable solutions. Indeed, where this principle is ignored, policymakers eventually are forced to return to it to succeed. Thus France, having imposed massive public housing projects on communities as a solution to nationwide housing shortages two decades ago, is busy today trying to foster local collaborative organizations to remedy the social and economic problems caused by that earlier decision. Thus too, the London Docklands Development Corporation, given extraordinary powers by central government to take over and redevelop a huge section of East London, has found it must work cooperatively with local governments, existing employers, schools, and others to meet its development objectives. Indeed, much of the LDDC's energies today are spent in remedying hostility created several years ago when it tried to impose its plans on the affected communities.

This is not to suggest that there is no role for national governments, but that national leadership is best exerted through broad policies developed cooperatively by government, labor, and industry. Implementation is best left to local partnerships. Both Britain's community schools and Philadelphia's WEPIC demonstrate that the strength of locally-crafted, community-relevant programs is not simply that everyone gets to contribute, but that everyone gains by contributing.

***Principle #7:*** *There are no "quick fixes" for building workforce competence; long-term investments and programmatic variety are vital.*

The West Philadelphia Improvement Corps is in its fourth year, and while its influence is spreading it is still predominantly a neighborhood-wide program. Given the intensity of school dropouts, crime, youth unemployment and related problems, the pace of change seems painfully slow. And yet, the participants have learned that patience is a virtue—that only by asking, planning, trying, evaluating, and trying again can permanent and workable solutions be found.

Many European nations have learned the same lesson. Their planning horizons are long-term, as are their investment commitments. Moreover, they have learned that there are no "silver bullets"—no sweeping, universally effective solutions. The barriers young people face in school and in the community are as varied as the young people themselves. What works for some does not for others; variety in education and training opportunities and flexibility in administration are therefore prerequisites of success. As a consequence, education and training initiatives in Europe tend to be highly "customer-oriented," rather than bureaucratic. In short, these countries continue to experiment and innovate, guided less by the dictates of the programs they have in place, than by what the customers—young people entering the workforce, adults already in the workforce, and the employers who hire them—need in order to be productive.

In the United States, the scattering of workforce-related programs among the U.S. Departments of Labor, Education, and Health and Human Services, among others—and the highly centralized administration of these programs—creates an institutionally-oriented, rather than a customer-oriented system, and one which often penalizes individuals who seek to escape dependency through training and education by eliminating or reducing their benefits before they have amassed sufficient earnings to achieve independence.

***Principle #8:*** *Compulsory schooling alone does not, and probably cannot, produce fully work-ready workers; everyone needs further education and training.*

To the extent that American policymakers at the national level have responded to the workforce competence issue, they have done so primarily by focusing on schools—pre-schools, primary, and secondary schools, in particular. In contrast, while many European countries expend significant resources annually to ensure the quality of their public schools, there is virtually universal recognition that a compulsory school education—even one which incorporates work orientation into the curriculum at an early age and provides work-related skill-building opportunities—is simply not enough to produce a work-ready labor market entrant. Additional, post-compulsory school training is vital.

In most European countries, there are clear paths to skills and economic opportunity for students leaving compulsory school and not going on to university. In Sweden, a three-year post-compulsory upper secondary school, where trade-specific skills are developed, has become virtually "compulsory" as far as employers are concerned. In West Germany, where apprenticeships are pursued by the vast majority of secondary school graduates, the part private, part public "dual system" is viewed by educators as an inherent part of the schooling system. In Britain, students completing compulsory school are strongly encouraged to stay on in school an additional year or two to attain higher qualifications, and to participate in two-year, nationally available post-graduation youth training schemes. In addition, "community schools" offer a wide range of further education opportunities at the neighborhood level.

The truth is that neither Europe nor Japan has any inherent edge on the United States in the struggle for global competitiveness. They earned the edge they currently hold by making sustained and significant investments in the education and skills of their citizens—all their citizens.

These are small nations, and perhaps as a consequence they are acutely aware of the capacity of the human resources they possess.

The United States on the other hand, accustomed as it is to abundance, has always assumed that resources will be available when needed. But a slowing birthrate and declining skill levels prove that, at least with respect to human resources, we can assume abundance no longer.

International leadership involves, at the most fundamental level, demonstrating the financial, social, intellectual, and political will to recreate in every individual, including the least advantaged, the spirit of what once was called "American Know-How"—the strength of purpose and conviction to succeed in a world far more competitive today than when that phrase was first coined.

There is little question that the energy and ideas characteristic of our pluralistic society—and embodied in local initiatives like the West Philadelphia Improvement Corps—can help us regain lost ground. What is in question is our ability to gather these ideas into a coherent national vision of workforce excellence and our willingness to redeploy resources to fulfill that vision.

One thing is unmistakably clear: how we resolve these questions will shape our role in the world for years to come.